# Kentucky's Best

# Kentucky's Best

## Fifty Years of Great Recipes

### Linda Allison-Lewis

THE UNIVERSITY PRESS OF KENTUCKY

Publication of this volume was made possible in part by a grant
from the National Endowment for the Humanities.

Published by The University Press of Kentucky
Scholarly publisher for the Commonwealth,
serving Bellarmine College, Berea College, Centre College of Kentucky,
Eastern Kentucky University, The Filson Club Historical Society,
Georgetown College, Kentucky Historical Society, Kentucky State University,
Morehead State University, Murray State University, Northern Kentucky University,
Transylvania University, University of Kentucky, University of Louisville,
and Western Kentucky University.

*Editorial and Sales Offices:* The University Press of Kentucky
663 South Limestone Street, Lexington, Kentucky 40508-4008

02 01 00 99 98    5 4 3 2 1

Cover photograph © 1998 by Jim Battles

"Green Pole Beans with Ham," "Chicken and Dumplings," "Beaten Biscuits," and "Jam Cake" by
Cissy Gregg. Copyright 1985 The Courier-Journal and Louisville Times Company. Reprinted
with permission.
"Oysters 'Louisville,'" "Special Mint Julep," and "Oaks Cheese Grits" from *That Special Touch* by
Sandra Davis
"Shaker Village Lemon Bread" from *Welcome Back to Pleasant Hill* by Elizabeth C. Kremer
"Chicken Salad with Country Dressing," "Cheese Wafers," and "Woodford Pudding with Vanilla
Sauce" from *We Make You Kindly Welcome* by Elizabeth C. Kremer
"Potato Croquettes," "Country Ham and Sausage Balls," "Candied Carrots," "Eggplant Casserole,"
"Country Ham Kentucky Style," "Mushrooms on Toast," "Egg Salad with Bacon and Country Ham,"
and "Sweet Potato Chips" from *Claudia Sanders Dinner House of Shelbyville, Kentucky, Cookbook* by
Cherry Settles, Tommy Settles, and Edward G. Klemm

Library of Congress Cataloging-in-Publication Data

Allison-Lewis, Linda, 1948-
    Kentucky's Best : fifty years of great recipes / Linda Allison-Lewis
        p.    cm.
    Includes index.
    ISBN 0-8131-2069-1 (cloth : alk. paper)
    1. Cookery, American. 2. Cookery—Kentucky. I. Title
YX715.A4429    1998
641.5—dc21                                98-39155

This book is printed on acid-free recycled paper meeting the requirements
of the American National Standard for Permanence of Paper for Printed Library Materials.

Manufactured in the United States of America

*To Noélle, Scott, Andrea, and Christian—*
*truly the best of my world*

# Contents

# Acknowledgments

Throughout the years many people have influenced and enhanced my love of fine food. My love of cooking began when I was taught to cook as a young child by my mother and my grandmothers. They taught me that any good dish is worth taking the time to ensure its success. For this I will always be grateful.

I am also thankful for the legacy Cissy Gregg left to me in all her work as Kentucky's best food columnist.

I thank the chefs and proprietors of the restaurants and bed-and-breakfast inns who graciously shared their recipes for this book; Charlotte and Michael Herron for their encouragement and much-needed technical help; and Judy, Linda, and Sue Ann, who shared with me the dream of Kentucky's best.

Most of all, I would like to thank my *Kentucky Living* readers and all the Kentucky cooks who send me great recipes along with wonderful stories. They are truly the inspiration for this book. If a recipe looks familiar, it probably is. More than likely the versions contained here evolved from a favorite of yours, an aunt's, or a daughter-in-law's. Please let them know how grateful I am and also how proud I am to live in a state whose cooks are second to none.

# Introduction

I grew up knowing that there was something very special about my home state and the tradition in cooking that my family enjoyed and encouraged. Several of my family members were entrepreneurs in the food business in Kentucky; they had been taught by old-world bakers. My grandparents owned a successful catering business during World War II and also operated many bakeries throughout the years. My uncle Vincent has served as pastry chef at such world-famous places as Boca Raton's five-star, five-diamond hotel, the Grand in Mackinaw Island, the French Lick Sheraton, and operations that serve Walt Disney World in Orlando. But despite his success throughout the country, he maintains today that the best cooks to be found anywhere are in his native Kentucky. He and I agree passionately on that point.

My memories of home include images of my mother and grandmother preparing Sunday dinner or planning menus for Derby guests. My grandmother was French. She was an avid reader of Cissy Gregg of the *Louisville Courier-Journal*. When she entertained, she created an air of elegance still found in many Kentucky homes today. She was the most confident cook I have ever known. She seemed to know as she would polish her silver or carefully select from fine table linens that the occasion would be a success because of the food she would serve. Her traditions and my impressions of her inspire me today as I enjoy cooking and working with food through my *Kentucky Living* column and preparing wonderful meals for my family and friends.

Many people think of a few of the same things when they think of Kentucky. Most are familiar with the Bluegrass region, which produces the greatest champion thoroughbred horses in the world, or the distilleries in Bardstown and Loretto, where the finest bourbon in the world is made. And many associate Kentucky with Daniel Boone, Abraham or Mary Todd Lincoln, Henry Clay, George Rogers Clark, and widely popular mountain folklore. The obvious success of burgoo, Owensboro barbecue, and Kentucky Fried Chicken is known to many still. But what we Kentucky cooks know is that our abilities and traditions have carried on for generations and continue to astound those who visit the Bluegrass state.

What also astounds those who visit Kentucky is the diversity of our cuisine. The true Kentucky traditional, rural foods are respected as much as the more elegant Kentucky cuisine. I know of no other state where Sunday fried chicken and homemade biscuits are anticipated as much as a delicate tiramisù. It is the diversity of the two as well as their blending that make Kentucky cuisine unique and very special. We truly have the best of both worlds.

We will visit many areas of Kentucky in this cookbook, offering recipes from great cooks across the state. Many wonderful recipes created by great Kentucky cooks are known only to their families and friends. We will sense true Kentucky pride while learning the culinary culture that is unique to the different areas of the state. We will visit the kitchens of my favorite Kentucky restaurants and bed-and-breakfast inns and learn of their favorite recipes.

All my life, I have loved entertaining and cooking: from gourmet foods to succulent Kentucky country ham with red-eye gravy and biscuits. I have worked as a restaurant critic in the great state of Texas. I have spent years watching my family carry on the traditions that my grandparents left me. What I have learned through all of this is what my uncle has known throughout his life as he has traveled this country cooking with some of the finest chefs in the world. The best cooks to be found anywhere are in Kentucky. We can all take pride in that!

# Kentucky's Best

# Appetizers

# Appetizers

 Each year a church in my community has a picnic featuring delicious chicken dinners, games, booths, and fun as a fund-raiser. The day before the picnic, it is tradition for the people who prepare the chicken to fry chicken livers for themselves. Once, many years ago, a strange thing happened to the livers. Someone mistook a huge bag of powdered sugar for flour. Dan Berry, a veteran fryer, told me that everyone looked at each other a little strangely when the first batch was sampled. "But," he added, "they were the best chicken livers ever!"

I know of no other category of food that I enjoy preparing more than appetizers. I can be as creative as I choose in preparing for parties at home as well as in making beautiful silver platters filled with delectable finger foods for my catering business. It is when I prepare appetizers that I most accomplish what the name of my small business—Impress the Guest—implies. I love watching my guests' eyes as they look over a table filled with spreads, fresh vegetables, dips, and surprise creations I always come up with at the last minute.

Every year on New Year's Eve my daughter, Noélle, and I have a standing tradition. I take her and several of her friends out to a very nice restaurant of their choice early in the evening. Afterwards the girls are invited back to the house to party: to make New Year's Eve decorations, to play with the karaoke machine, to snack on appetizers throughout the night, and to sleep over. Noélle and her best friend, Andi, ages thirteen and twelve, enjoy this tradition tremendously and always look forward to the big tray of "grown-up food" I put out for them. Even kids enjoy the sophistication of party foods presented in a creative way.

Appetizers can be made from many ingredients. I feature here Oysters "Louisville," compliments of Maker's Mark Distillery in Loretto, Kentucky, and author Sandra Davis, which will certainly win raves from the men at any party. Crabmeat Fingers and Cashew-Curry Spread are also great selections. Remember, appetizers are not only foods to whet one's appetite for a great entrée; with a little creativity and the freshest ingredients, they can stand on their own to create a memorable occasion at any party.

# ❧ BARBECUED PECANS ❧

4 cups pecan halves

3 tablespoons margarine, melted

1 tablespoon salt

3 tablespoons Worcestershire sauce

½ teaspoon ground cinnamon

¼ teaspoon cayenne

Dash of Tabasco

Preheat oven to 325 degrees. Mix pecans with margarine and salt. Add Worcestershire sauce, cinnamon, cayenne, and Tabasco, mixing well. Spread mixture onto cookie sheet. Stirring occasionally, bake for 15 minutes, or until brown and margarine is absorbed.

*Yield:* 4 cups
*Note:* These freeze well.

# ❧ BEER CHEESE ❧

10 ounces grated Cracker Barrel sharp cheddar cheese

10 ounces grated Cracker Barrel mild cheddar cheese

2 cloves garlic, minced

3 green onions with tops, finely chopped

¼ teaspoon cayenne

½ teaspoon Tabasco

¾ cup stale beer

Soften cheese in microwave. Combine all ingredients and mix until blended. Cover and store in a bowl in refrigerator. Mixture will harden after being chilled. Set out and allow to reach room temperature before serving.

*Yield:* 2 cups
*Note:* This cheese tastes better the longer it sits. Serve with crackers.

# OLIVE CHEESE BALL

½ pound sharp cheddar cheese, grated (2 cups)
1¼ cups all-purpose flour
¼ pound (1 stick) margarine, softened
36 small pimiento-stuffed green olives, drained

Mix cheese and flour with margarine (work dough with hands if it seems dry). Mold 1 teaspoon dough around each olive. Shape into ball. Place 2 inches apart on ungreased cookie sheet. Cover and refrigerate for at least 1 hour. Preheat oven to 400 degrees. Bake for 15 to 20 minutes.

*Yield:* 10 to 12 servings

# CHEESE-CHUTNEY PÂTÉ

1 (3-ounce) package cream cheese, softened
2 ounces sharp cheddar cheese, grated (½ cup)
2 teaspoons dry sherry
¼ teaspoon curry powder
⅛ teaspoon salt
¾ cup chutney
Finely chopped green onions with tops

Combine cream cheese, cheddar cheese, sherry, curry powder, and salt and beat until smooth.

Shape mixture into ½-inch-thick circle. Chill until firm. Spread chutney over top and sprinkle with green onions.

*Yield:* 1 cup
*Note:* Serve with crackers.

# BENEDICTINE SPREAD

*So many Kentuckians are grateful to Miss Jennie Benedict, a Louisville caterer, for creating Benedictine spread before the turn of the century. I grew up enjoying this famous green spread when my family would entertain. My mother would order green and pink loaves of bread from the bakery. She would cut off the crusts, slice the bread thin, and fill the green loaves with pimiento cheese and the pink loaves with this great Benedictine. These finger sandwiches were so colorful at her parties and club nights. I love my version, but admit that a dash of Tabasco added to the mixture makes it even better.*

1 (8-ounce) package cream cheese, softened

1 tablespoon mayonnaise

3 tablespoons grated cucumber, drained well with paper towel

1 teaspoon finely chopped green onions with tops

1 drop green food coloring

Blend all ingredients together and mix well.

*Yield:* 10 to 12 servings
*Note:* Serve as dip or use as spread for finger sandwiches.


# CASHEW-CURRY SPREAD

4 to 5 ounces cream cheese

½ cup cottage cheese

1 teaspoon curry powder

½ cup finely chopped cashews

Mash cheeses together. Add curry powder and cashews. Mix together and chill for at least 1 hour.

*Yield:* 4 servings    *Note:* Serve with crackers.

# ✆ OYSTER SPREAD ✆

2 (8-ounce) packages cream cheese, softened

¼ cup milk

2 to 3 tablespoons mayonnaise

1 tablespoon lemon juice

1 tablespoon Worcestershire sauce

Dash of hot sauce

¼ teaspoon salt

2 (6-ounce) cans smoked oysters, finely chopped

Paprika

Chopped fresh parsley

Combine all ingredients except oysters, paprika, and parsley. Blend well. Stir in oysters and refrigerate several hours. Sprinkle with paprika and parsley before serving.

*Yield:* 3 cups

# ✆ PIMIENTO, CREAM CHEESE, ✆ AND PECAN SPREAD

2 (8-ounce) packages cream cheese, softened

1 (4-ounce) jar pimientos with liquid

Dash of pepper

1 tablespoon sugar

⅓ tablespoon salt

1½ tablespoons flour

1 egg, well beaten

¼ cup white vinegar

4 tablespoons (½ stick) butter, melted

1 cup chopped pecans

Beat cream cheese, pimientos with liquid, and pepper with electric mixer until well blended. Mix sugar, salt, flour, egg, and vinegar in small saucepan. Add melted butter and cook over medium heat until thick. Pour into cream cheese mixture and beat until well mixed. Add pecans, mix well, and chill.

*Yield:* 2 cups
*Note:* Serve with crackers.

## ❧ STRAWBERRY BUTTER ❧

*One of my favorites during strawberry season is the following. I serve this with banana bread or banana muffins. It is a wonderful summer treat.*

¾ cup mashed strawberries
½ pound (2 sticks) unsalted butter, softened

Mix ingredients together.

*Yield:* 1¾ cups
*Note:* Serve at room temperature.

# PICO DE GALLO

*I prefer this to salsa when serving chips, quesadillas, and most Mexican dishes. I use it to top southwest casseroles and Tex-Mex dishes.*

4 ripe tomatoes, chopped

1 medium onion, chopped

¼ cup finely chopped jalapeño peppers, with juice

4 cloves garlic, minced

1 tablespoon fresh chopped cilantro, if possible (dried will do)

A few drops of lime juice

Mix all ingredients together and store in jar in refrigerator.

*Yield:* 2 cups

# POTATO CROQUETTES

Claudia Sanders Dinner House of Shelbyville, Kentucky, Cookbook *by Cherry Settles, Tommy Settles, and Edward G. Klemm*

*These potato croquettes make an excellent appetizer when made in a small size.*

1 egg yolk

1½ tablespoons butter, melted

1 teaspoon light cream

½ teaspoon salt

⅛ teaspoon pepper

¼ teaspoon celery salt

¼ teaspoon onion juice

2¼ cups riced cooked potatoes

½ cup coarse saltine cracker crumbs

Fat or corn oil for deep frying

Beat egg yolk. Add melted butter, cream, salt, pepper, celery salt, and onion juice. Stir to mix thoroughly. Add potatoes and whip mixture to combine. Heat fat or corn oil for deep frying to 390 degrees (using cooking thermometer). Shape croquettes by rolling rounded tablespoons (or teaspoons, if making appetizers) of mixture into balls and then flattening them slightly to get desired effect. Roll in cracker crumbs. Deep fry for at least 1 minute. Remove from fat and drain.

*Yield:* 18 to 20 croquettes

# ∞ COUNTRY HAM AND ∞ SAUSAGE BALLS

Claudia Sanders Dinner House of Shelbyville, Kentucky, Cookbook *by Cherry Settles, Tommy Settles, and Edward G. Klemm*

1 pound ground Claudia Sanders Kentucky Country Ham

½ pound pork sausage

½ cup finely ground cheese- and garlic-flavored croutons

1 egg, beaten

5 drops onion juice

⅓ cup milk

15 ounces prepared spaghetti sauce

Preheat oven to 400 degrees. Mix all ingredients together, blending thoroughly. Roll into bite-size balls. Place balls in baking pan large enough to hold them without touching each other. Pour sauce over meatballs. Bake for 1 hour, or until meatballs are firm.

*Yield:* 4 to 5 dozen

# CRABMEAT FINGERS

½ cup tomato juice
1 egg, well beaten
1 cup dried fine bread crumbs
¼ teaspoon black pepper
Dash of salt
¼ teaspoon crushed red pepper
½ teaspoon chopped parsley
½ teaspoon chopped celery leaves
1 (6½-ounce) can crabmeat, flaked
12 slices bacon, halved

Preheat broiler. Combine tomato juice and egg. Add bread crumbs, seasonings, parsley, celery leaves, and crabmeat and mix thoroughly. Roll into finger lengths. Wrap each roll with ½ slice bacon and fasten with toothpick. Broil, turning frequently, until evenly browned.

*Yield:* 1 dozen rolls

# OYSTERS "LOUISVILLE"

*Maker's Mark Distillery*
*From* That Special Touch *by Sandra Davis*

Slices of bacon, halved
Raw oysters
Sliced or halved water chestnuts
Maker's Mark Gourmet Sauce

Wrap slice of bacon around each oyster with a piece of water chestnut in it and secure with toothpicks. Pour Gourmet Sauce over oysters and broil until bacon is cooked on one side; turn and broil other side.

*Yield:* 8 to 10 servings    *Note:* Serve hot.

# FRIED BANANA PEPPERS

1 15-ounce jar hot banana peppers (or use fresh if available)
1½ cups milk
1 egg, lightly beaten
½ can beer
1½ cups flour
½ cup finely ground saltine cracker crumbs
Vegetable oil or shortening for frying

Split peppers and seed. In one bowl, combine milk, egg, and beer. In second bowl, put 1 cup of the flour. In third bowl, combine cracker crumbs and remaining ½ cup flour. Dip peppers into milk mixture and coat with flour. Set aside for 10 minutes. Dip peppers again into milk and coat with cracker crumb mixture. Refrigerate for 15 minutes. Heat vegetable oil or shortening in deep fryer. Drop peppers in hot shortening and fry until medium brown. Drain and serve.

*Yield:* 4 servings

# HOT ARTICHOKE DIP

*I serve this dish when I cater. Even though it is an older recipe, it is still the first dish to empty. Guests love it even when they don't think they like artichokes!*

1 (14-ounce) can artichoke hearts, drained and chopped
1 cup mayonnaise
4 ounces Parmesan cheese, grated (1 cup)
Dash of garlic powder

Preheat oven to 350 degrees. Combine all ingredients and pour into ungreased 1-1½-quart casserole. Bake for 35 to 40 minutes, or until golden brown and bubbly.

*Yield:* 10 to 12 servings    *Note:* Serve with corn chips and crackers.

# ARTICHOKE SQUARES

*Harralson House Inn Bed and Breakfast*

*The Harralson House Inn Bed and Breakfast, located in Princeton, Kentucky, offers an ambiance of impeccable taste, more genteel days, and a commitment to peace and tranquillity by owner Lois Hall Wilson. Lois offers truly wonderful dishes such as this salad to her guests.*

2 (6-ounce) jars marinated artichokes with liquid

1 small onion, chopped

1 clove garlic, minced

½ pound cheddar cheese, grated (2 cups)

4 eggs, well beaten

½ teaspoon dried oregano

1 cup fine dry seasoned bread crumbs

Salt and pepper to taste

Preheat oven to 350 degrees. Reserving liquid from 1 jar, drain and chop artichokes. Pour liquid into pan and sauté onion and garlic until soft. Mix all other ingredients with artichokes and pour into 8 x 8-inch pan. Bake for 30 to 40 minutes. Cut into squares.

*Yield:* 16 squares
*Note:* Serve hot or cold.

# Breads and Rolls

# Bread and Rolls

 During the years of my marriage I was blessed with a mother-in-law, Flossie Fulkerson Lewis, who was a true friend and an inspiration. I recall a Sunday afternoon a year or so before her death when the entire family was coming over for Sunday dinner. I walked into the kitchen, sat down across from her, and said, "What's for dessert? It smells wonderful."

"Chocolate cake," she replied, looking as though she had died the death of a rag doll, lifeless and airless.

"What's wrong?" I asked.

"I think I forgot to put in the eggs," she answered.

I got up from my chair and peeped into the oven. Sure enough, the cake was flat as a pancake. About that time her son came walking through the door and hollered, "What's for dessert? It smells great."

I looked at him, smiled, and said, "Brownies," closing the oven door.

Flossie smiled, too.

This chapter is exciting for me because it contains bread recipes that my uncle Vincent and I created using home breadmakers. These machines are quite popular today and are becoming more and more affordable. I chose several of the best recipes we tested and included them in this section for those of you fortunate enough to have a breadmaker. I use mine quite frequently in colder months and enjoy the convenience of homemade bread without the work. And nothing on earth compares to the smell of bread baking in the oven. My daughter, Noélle, and I often enjoy a meal of homemade bread and a pot of homemade soup—truly one of my favorite meals.

The best bread I have ever eaten is the Buttermilk Bread for the Home Breadmaker, which can also be made the conventional way. I always bring mine up to the dough mode on my machine and then bake it in a traditional loaf pan. I prefer the shape of a loaf. My son Scott loves this bread also. Years ago while living in Texas and working on these recipes long distance with my uncle, I would make it on a daily basis. Scott would come in from school with his friends, break open the loaf, grab huge hunks of bread, and eat it while it was still warm. I can still see the big grin on his face as he spread butter on a piece of bread rich enough to be eaten plain.

The Harralson House Inn Bed and Breakfast in Princeton, Kentucky, offers us its Refrigerator Yeast Biscuits, which are absolutely delicious. The Shaker Village Lemon Bread from the Shaker Village, located in Pleasant Hill, Kentucky, doubles as a nice lunch treat, and my own Clean-Up-the-Garden Bread was actually created out of an effort to use up leftover vegetables in a backyard garden I once tended. Perhaps the most exciting thing in this category is the Sourmash Bourbon Bread debuted by Executive Chef Jim Gerhardt of Louisville's Seelbach Hotel at the James Beard Foundation in New York City in May 1997. This is truly a contribution all Kentuckians can be proud of.

Bread is called the staff of life. I hope you spice up your menus with some of my favorites.

# BUTTERMILK BREAD FOR THE HOME BREADMAKER

*This bread has an excellent, velvety texture, and no other bread we tested smelled as good as this one while baking. It is definitely my favorite breadmaker recipe.*

1 cup buttermilk, heated until milk coats a spoon, then cooled

2½ cups bread flour

4 tablespoons sugar

½ teaspoon salt

¼ teaspoon baking soda

4 tablespoons (½ stick) unsalted butter (no substitutions)

1½ teaspoons active dry yeast

Put ingredients in breadmaker in order listed. Proceed according to manufacturer's instructions. If more flour is needed after mixing begins, add 1 tablespoon at a time to make stiff dough.

*Yield:* 1 loaf

# ❧ DILLY PRETZELS ❧
## FOR THE HOME BREADMAKER

1 cup warm water

2½ cups bread flour

1 teaspoon sugar

½ teaspoon salt

1½ teaspoons active dry yeast

1½ teaspoons dried dill

1 beaten egg

coarse salt

Put first six ingredients in breadmaker in order listed. Proceed according to manufacturer's instructions until the dough cycle is completed. Preheat oven to 450 degrees. Divide dough into 15 pieces. Shape into pretzels or twist into 7-inch strips. Brush with beaten egg wash and sprinkle with coarse salt. Bake for 15 minutes.

*Yield:* 15 pretzels or strips

*Note:* These pretzels are excellent with mustard or hot Swiss dip, which is made with ½ cup grated Swiss cheese, ¼ cup of milk, and 1 teaspoon of dijon mustard melted together in microwave.

# DILLY RYE BREAD
## FOR THE HOME BREADMAKER

1 cup warm water

1¼ cups bread flour

1¼ cups rye flour

1 tablespoon dry skim milk

1 tablespoon sugar

1 teaspoon salt

1 tablespoon caraway seeds

1 tablespoon freshly snipped dill

1 tablespoon butter or margarine

1½ teaspoons active dry yeast

Put ingredients in bread machine in order listed. Proceed according to manufacturer's instructions. If more flour is needed after mixing begins, add 1 tablespoon at a time.

*Yield:* 1 loaf

# PUMPERKNICKEL BREAD
## FOR THE HOME BREADMAKER

1 cup warm water

1¼ cups bread flour

1¼ cups rye flour

1 tablespoon dry skim milk

2 tablespoons molasses

1 teaspoon salt

1 tablespoon caraway seeds

1½ teaspoons cocoa

1 tablespoon butter or margarine

1½ teaspoons active dry yeast

Put ingredients in breadmaker in order listed. Proceed according to manufacturer's instructions. If more flour is needed after mixing begins, add 1 tablespoon at a time.

*Yield:* 1 loaf

# SAVORY BRIOCHE
# FOR THE HOME BREADMAKER

¼ cup warm water

½ cup melted butter

2 eggs, lightly beaten

¼ teaspoon Dijon mustard

2 cups all-purpose flour

ground black pepper

1 teaspoon sugar

¼ teaspoon salt

½ cup grated Gruyere cheese

1½ teaspoons active dry yeast

Add ingredients to breadmaker in order listed. Proceed according to manufacturer's instructions.

*Yield:* 1 loaf

# WHEAT AND HONEY LOAF
# FOR THE HOME BREADMAKER

¼ cup warm water

2 tablespoons oil

¼ cup honey

½ cup 2 percent milk (warm, approximately 200 degrees)

1¼ cups bread flour

1¼ cups whole wheat flour

1 tablespoon butter or margarine

1 tablespoon sugar

1 teaspoon salt

1½ teaspoons active dry yeast

Add ingredients to breadmaker in order listed. Proceed according to manufacturer's instructions. If more flour is needed after mixing begins, add 1 tablespoon at a time.

*Yield:* 1 loaf

# CLEAN-UP-THE-GARDEN BREAD

*This bread is so moist and delicious. You'll love it!*

3 eggs

1 cup vegetable oil

1½ cups sugar

1 cup grated zucchini

1 cup grated carrots

1 cup grated yellow squash

½ cup drained pineapple chunks

3 cups all-purpose flour

½ cup chopped walnuts

1 teaspoon baking powder

1 teaspoon baking soda

2 teaspoons salt

1 teaspoon ground cinnamon

Preheat oven to 325 degrees. Beat eggs with oil, sugar, and grated vegetables. Add pineapple chunks. Add flour, walnuts, baking powder, baking soda, salt, and cinnamon. Pour into two greased 9 x 5 x 3-inch loaf pans and bake for 1 hour.

*Yield:* Two 9 x 5 x 3-inch loaves

# MY FAVORITE OATMEAL BREAD

1½ teaspoon active dry yeast

¾ cup warm water (110 degrees)

1½ cups old-fashioned rolled oats (not instant or quick)

¼ cup plus 1 tablespoon solid vegetable shortening

¼ cup sugar

2½ teaspoons salt

1 cup milk

3 to 3½ cups bread flour

1 egg, lightly beaten

Dissolve yeast in half of the warm water. In large bowl, combine oats, shortening, sugar, and salt. Heat milk until it coats a spoon and pour over oat mixture. Let stand several minutes, stirring twice. Add remaining warm water to oat mixture and cool to lukewarm. Beat in 1 cup of flour, egg, and yeast. Add enough of remaining flour to make stiff dough. Knead on lightly floured surface until smooth, 12 to 15 minutes. Shape into ball and place in greased bowl. Turn once. Cover and allow to rise in a warm place at approximately 200 degrees Farenheit until doubled in size.

Punch down dough and let rest, covered, about 12 minutes. Grease metal loaf pan. Roll out dough to form large triangle. Roll up like jellyroll, beginning at short end. Pinch and press sides under to seal. Place loaf seam side down in pan. Cover loaf and let rise until doubled in size. Preheat oven to 375 degrees and bake about 50 minutes or until loaf is golden brown and sounds hollow when bottom is tapped. Remove from pan and cool on wire rack.

*Yield:* 1 loaf

# RHUBARB BREAD

**Bread**

1½ cups light brown sugar (packed)

⅔ cup vegetable oil

1 egg

1 cup sour milk

1 teaspoon vanilla

1 teaspoon salt

1 teaspoon soda

2½ cups flour

1½ cups finely diced rhubarb

½ cup chopped nuts

**Topping**

½ cup light brown sugar (packed)

½ teaspoon cinnamon

1 tablespoon butter, softened

Preheat oven to 325 degrees. Combine brown sugar and oil. Stir in sour milk and vanilla. (Start with whole or 2 percent milk. Sour by adding 1 teaspoon vinegar.) Sift dry ingredients together and add. Stir in rhubarb and nuts. Pour into 2 well-greased loaf pans. Combine brown sugar, cinnamon, and butter and sprinkle on top. Bake for 40 minutes. Cool in pan.

*Yield:* 1 loaf

# SHAKER VILLAGE OF PLEASANT HILL LEMON BREAD

*Shaker Village of Pleasant Hill*

*From* Welcome Back to Pleasant Hill *by Elizabeth C. Kremer*

### Bread

⅓ cup shortening

1 cup granulated sugar

2 eggs

1½ cups all-purpose flour, sifted

1½ teaspoons baking powder

¼ teaspoon salt

½ cup milk

Grated rind of 1 lemon

½ cup nuts, chopped (optional)

Beat together shortening and sugar until light and fluffy. Add eggs, one at a time, beating well after each. Sift dry ingredients and add alternately with milk to sugar mixture, beating well after each addition. Add lemon rind and nuts if desired. Turn into one greased large loaf pan or two small ones. Bake in 350-degree oven for about 60 minutes.

### Glaze

⅓ cup granulated sugar

Juice of 1 lemon

Mix together and pour over bread immediately after removing from oven.

*Yield:* 1 to 2 loaves

# SOUTHERN SPOON BREAD

1 cup yellow corn meal

1½ teaspoons baking powder

½ teaspoon salt

2¼ cups milk

2 eggs, beaten

2 tablespoons butter, melted (optional)

Preheat oven to 425 degrees. Stir together corn meal, baking powder, and salt. In medium-size pan, heat milk (stir to avoid scorching). As it starts boiling, sprinkle in dry ingredients, stirring vigorously with wooden spoon. Cook and stir for 2 to 3 minutes, as it thickens. Pour into greased casserole, add eggs, and mix. Bake for 45 minutes. Drizzle butter on top after baking if desired. Serve from casserole with spoon.

*Yield:* 6 servings

# CRACKLIN CORN BREAD

½ cup cornmeal

½ cup all-purpose flour

2 teaspoons baking powder

½ teaspoon salt

1 egg, beaten

1½ cups milk

½ cup crackling (see note)

Preheat oven to 400 degrees. Sift together cornmeal, flour, baking powder, and salt. In another bowl, combine egg, milk, and cracklings. Combine with cornmeal mixture. Beat well and pour into hot, greased iron skillet. Bake until brown and a toothpick inserted in the center comes out clean.

*Yield:* 8 servings

*Note:* Crackling are the crisp bits left in the fat after meat is fried.

# THE DEPOT'S FLOWERPOT WHITE BREAD

*The Depot*

*The Depot Restaurant, located in Glendale, Kentucky, near Elizabethtown, serves the most wonderful bread in flowerpots. I always eat too much bread and fill up before my dinner is served. It's addictive!*

*Glendale is one of my favorite towns because visitors can dine at the Depot Restaurant or the Whistle Stop (located at opposite ends of the railroad tracks) and be assured of enjoying some of Kentucky's best home cooking. The town also boasts wonderful antique shops in which to browse after enjoying a great meal. Some of my most memorable afternoons have been spent there.*

1 pkg active dry yeast

¼ cup warm water (110 to 115 degrees)

2 cups whole or 2 percent milk

2 tablespoons sugar

1 tablespoon shortening

2 teaspoons salt

5¾ to 6¼ cups all-purpose flour

Melted butter

4 (4-inch) clay flowerpots

Soften yeast in warm water. In saucepan heat milk, sugar, shortening, and salt just until warm (115 to 120 degrees) and shortening is almost melted. Stir constantly. Turn into large mixing bowl. Stir in 2 cups of the flour and beat well. Add softened yeast and stir until smooth. Stir in as much of remaining flour as needed to make moderately stiff dough that is smooth and elastic (6 to 8 minutes). Shape into ball. Place in lightly greased bowl and turn once to grease surface. Cover and let rise in a warm place at approximately 200 degrees Farenheit until double in size (about 1½ hours).

Punch down and divide into 4 equal pieces of dough and shape into small balls. Place balls into lightly greased flowerpots. (I season my clean flowerpots prior to using by greasing generously with shortening and allowing the empty pots to bake in the oven at about 300 degrees for 1 hour). Set in warm place and let rise until about 1½ inches over top of pots.

Preheat oven to 350 degrees. Put pots on cookie sheet and slide into oven. Bake for 25 to 35 minutes or until bread comes out of pots easily. Butter tops with melted butter, using pastry brush. Remove from pots and serve immediately.

*Yield:* 4 loaves

## POTATO BISCUITS

1 cup mashed potatoes

2 tablespoons butter, softened

½ teaspoon soda

1 cup buttermilk

1 tablespoon honey

2 cups all-purpose flour

1 teaspoon salt

2 teaspoons baking powder

1 tablespoon light brown sugar (packed)

Preheat oven to 400 degrees. Stir butter into potatoes. Dissolve soda in buttermilk and add honey. Mix baking powder, sugar, flour, and salt and add to buttermilk mixture. Combine with potatoes. Press dough into ¾-inch-thick circle. Cut biscuits with biscuit cutter. Bake for 8 to 10 minutes or until brown.

*Yield:* 12 biscuits

# SOURMASH
# BOURBON BREAD

*The Oakroom of the Seelbach Hotel*

*This is one of the best breads I've ever eaten. Executive Chef
Jim Gerhardt of the Seelbach, in his search for an original
"Kentucky Fine Dining Bread," has teamed up with Early Times
Bourbon Whiskey to create the ultimate Sourmash Bourbon Bread.
The rich mixture of corn, barley, and wheat with its delicate
bourbon nuances and century-old sourmash yeast strain makes an
exceptional Kentucky version of San Francisco sourdough. I used a
breadmaker for the following recipe and the results were excellent.
The bread can be purchased in French loaves at the Seelbach or the
mix can be ordered and shipped anywhere in the world
simply by calling the Seelbach Hotel in Louisville.*

Mix 1 cup Bourbon Flour with 2 cups tepid water and 1 teaspoon
vegetable oil in a large stainless steel bowl. Add 2 cups all purpose flour,
3 teaspoons sugar, 1 teaspoon sorghum/molasses and 3 teaspoons dry
instant yeast.

Thoroughly mix. Let rest 5 minutes. With 1 cup all purpose flour
on side, knead, adding flour as needed until dough is not sticky and is
soft, smooth and elastic. Let rise for 10-20 minutes. Brush with egg
wash (½ egg white, ½ water mixed), cut ½ inch deep X in top for air
vents and bake in oiled and cornmeal sprinkled French bread pan or pie
pan until golden brown, 35-40 minutes at 350 degrees.

*Note:* This makes a very large loaf of bread. Enjoy!

# REFRIGERATOR ∞ YEAST BISCUITS

*Harralson House Inn Bed and Breakfast*

1½ teaspoons active dry yeast

¼ cup warm water (110 degrees)

2 tablespoons sugar

5 cups all-purpose flour

1 tablespoon baking powder

1 teaspoon baking soda

1 teaspoon salt

1 cup vegetable shortening

2 cups buttermilk, warmed

Dissolve yeast in the warm water with one tablespoon of sugar and set aside. Mix flour and one tablespoon sugar, baking powder, soda, and salt. Add shortening and mix until mixture resembles coarse meal. Add yeast mixture and buttermilk. Mix until dry ingredients are moistened. Pour into lightly greased bowl, cover, and refrigerate until needed.

Turn dough out onto greased, floured surface and knead lightly 4 to 5 times. Roll dough to ½-inch thickness and cut with 2-inch biscuit cutter. Dip in melted butter and place on greased baking sheet. Let rise in warm place at approximately 200 degrees Farenheit for about 1 hour, covered with towel. (I suggest letting the dough sit in a 200-degree oven with a pan of hot water and the oven door closed.) Preheat oven to 450 degrees and bake until browned, about 12 to 15 minutes.

*Yield:* about 2 dozen

# ✍ JIFFY ROLLS ✍

*This is an excellent make-and-serve roll.*

3 teaspoons active dry yeast

1 cup warm water (110 degrees)

⅓ cup salad oil

1½ tablespoons sugar

1½ teaspoons salt

1 egg, well beaten

3 to 3½ cups all-purpose flour

¼ cup melted butter

Dissolve yeast in warm water. Stir in oil, sugar, salt, and egg. Stir in flour, one cup at a time, until soft dough is formed. Turn onto lightly floured surface; knead until smooth, adding small amounts of flour as needed to keep dough from being sticky. Cover with clean towel and let rest 15 minutes. Roll dough into rectangle, brush with melted butter, and roll up as jelly roll. Slice into pieces about 1 inch thick. Place the pieces in buttered muffin tins, cover, and let rise in a warm place at approximately 200 degrees for thirty minutes.

Preheat oven to 400 degrees and bake 10 to 12 minutes, until lightly browned. Brush with melted butter.

*Yield:* 1½ to 2 dozen

# Side Dishes

# Side Dishes

 Twenty-five years ago Jessica Neal, three years old at the time and definitely in the chatty stage, would visit her grandmother, Rose Morgan, in Meade County, Kentucky. Rose was a fine Kentucky cook who loved to cook for company, field hands who worked the hay on her farm, or anyone who happened to stop by and partake of her groaning board.

Young Jessica would stand on a chair to see what Grandma Rose put in her turkey gravy.

"What goes in the gravy, Grandma?" she would demand to know. "What are you putting in it?"

Rose Morgan was determined not to let Jessica see the giblets she would chop up and add to the pan, for fear her granddaughter would quit eating the gravy. Finally she would tell her, "It's tiny fish, Jessica. I put them in so you can catch them." Young Jessica never stopped eating giblet gravy.

Side dishes are quite an opportunity to be creative with food. A side dish, while meant to complement and not compete with an entrée, can take the form of casserole, sautéed vegetables, potatoes, or pasta.

The most exciting time for me to prepare side dishes is when my favorite vegetables are in season. A platter of ripe tomatoes sliced fresh from the garden can complement a meal as well as candied carrots or a fancy eggplant dish.

I feature several vegetable recipes from my *Kentucky Living* column given to me by Fred and Jenny Wiche. Fred Wiche is Kentucky's best-known gardener, and these delicious side dishes show that he and his wife, Jenny, are quite skilled in the kitchen, too. The Asparagus Parmesan is a favorite of mine.

Shady Lane Bed and Breakfast Inn's Green Fried Tomatoes are the best I have tasted, and it is true that one should use green tomatoes with only a tinge of pink or they become soft when fried. Brodrick's Tavern offers us a corn pudding that is as much Kentucky as any recipe in this book. And the Turnip Greens with Cornmeal Dumplings continues to be a dish that I prepare often.

Use your imagination to prepare exciting side dishes that win raves.

# BAKED BEANS

*My mother makes the best baked beans I've ever eaten, and I'm including her recipe here. They're always a hit at get-togethers, and a picnic wouldn't be the same without them. They're spicy and equally good hot or cold.*

2 (15-ounce) cans pork and beans

1 cup light brown sugar

¼ cup cider vinegar

¾ cup ketchup

½ cup smoke-flavored barbecue sauce

4 slices uncooked bacon, cut into pieces

Preheat oven to 400 degrees. Mix together beans, brown sugar, vinegar, ketchup, and barbecue sauce. Pour into 13 x 9 x 2-inch glass baking dish. Lay bacon pieces over top and bake for 35 to 40 minutes, until bubbly.

*Yield:* 8 servings

# &#10086; MY FAVORITE &#10086;
## BUTTER BEANS

*This is one of my favorite recipes. When I was young, I remember my aunt Ruth serving wonderful pots of butter beans. I still believe none others are as good as hers, but I come as close as possible with this recipe. I like to cook the beans slowly for hours on a cold afternoon. I consider them to be a great comfort food, and they always win raves from family and friends.*

1 pound large lima beans

Cold water

½ pound (2 sticks) unsalted butter (no substitutions)

1 cup half-and-half

Salt and pepper

Rinse and sort beans in large bowl, cover them with cold water, and let them soak for 2 hours. Drain and transfer to large Dutch oven. Cover with cold water and bring to a boil. Add butter and continue cooking slowly until beans are tender, stirring occasionally. When liquid is mostly absorbed and beans are tender, add half-and-half. Continue simmering 20 minutes longer. Add salt and pepper to taste.

*Yield:* 12 servings

# GREEN POLE BEANS ✇ WITH HAM

*Cissy Gregg,* Louisville Courier-Journal

*This Cissy Gregg recipe dates back to 1950. Maybe we get a more tender variety of pole beans at the supermarket these days, because many cooks use only a fraction of Cissy's cooking time on their beans. "Hull-outs" are shelled beans. Cooking green beans in ham liquor is more like a "way" with the two foods than a recipe.*

Buy the size of ham hock that will not make too ghastly a hole in your budget. Ours was a good-sized one, but that isn't necessary. Put the ham hock in a kettle of water. The water should almost cover the meat. However, the size of your kettle and the amount of beans you are using make a difference. The idea is to hit on the amount of water that will serve for the ham, then the beans, leaving only about a cup of liquor at the finish. Cover and simmer the ham until tender. I prefer the ham to be minus the bean flavor, and cook the beans only in the liquor. But that is a personal matter. Also consider the time element.

Take the cooked ham out of the kettle. Have ready 4 pounds of green pole beans and 1 pound of hull-outs. Have the pole beans washed, strung, and broken into suitable lengths. Drop these into the boiling ham broth along with a pod of red pepper. Cover, and when the broth comes to a boil, turn the fire down so the beans will do no more than quietly simmer along. The water can become a little gay but not boisterous. If beans are boiled rapidly and water added they are never as good. Rapid cooking tears the beans open and causes them to be stringy. Keep the water going at the speed where it will not have to be renewed. The usual time given to cooking green beans hangs around 2 to 3 hours. Salt can be added toward the last, and the amount must depend on the flavor of the ham. Don't oversalt beans or any vegetable since it has a way of robbing the flavor. There is a staunch divided opinion on when to add the hull-outs. My preference goes with those who add them after the pole beans have been cooking about an hour, since I like the hull-outs to be soft, all right, but not mushy. Others start them about the same time.

# A KENTUCKY POT OF GREENS

*Great Kentucky cooks often rely on a pot of greens to round out a menu. Cooked in true Kentucky fashion, these greens have become a staple in our cuisine. Pick your favorite greens and enjoy.*

1 pound kale greens

1 pound turnip greens

½ pound collard greens

2 cups country ham pieces

2 quarts water

Salt and pepper

Wash greens and tear large leaves from stems (especially kale). Put leaves, ham, and water in large Dutch oven and bring to a boil. Boil 5 minutes and reduce heat to simmer. Cook until desired tenderness. Salt and pepper to taste. Reserve liquid to serve in bowl for dipping cornbread.

*Yield:* 8 servings

# ❧ TURNIP GREENS ❧ WITH CORNMEAL DUMPLINGS

About 1 pound ham hocks

2 quarts water

1 bunch turnip greens and roots (3 to 4 pounds)

Dash of pepper

1 cup cornmeal

1 teaspoon sugar

½ teaspoon salt

1½ cups water

1 egg, beaten

About ½ cup flour

Wash ham hocks and put in 8-quart Dutch oven. Add the water and bring to a boil. Reduce heat and simmer for 40 minutes, or until meat is tender.

Check turnip greens carefully; remove pulpy stems and discolored spots on leaves. Wash turnip greens and roots thoroughly; drain well. Chop turnip greens; peel turnip roots and cut in half. Add turnip greens, roots, and pepper to Dutch oven; bring to a boil. Cover, reduce heat, and simmer for about 50 minutes, or until greens and roots are tender.

Combine cornmeal, sugar, and salt; mix well. Bring 1½ cups water to a boil in saucepan and stir in cornmeal mixture. Remove from heat. Add egg and mix well. Drop cornmeal mixture by tablespoonfuls onto floured board and roll in flour. Drop dumplings into water over turnip greens; cover and cook over medium heat for 15 minutes.

*Yield:* 8 to 10 servings

# APPLE BUTTER-PUMPKIN FRITTERS

*This is a great fall comfort food. And who doesn't love apple butter on a cold morning? The apple butter adds such zest to this recipe.*

Vegetable oil for frying

1 cup unsifted flour

1½ teaspoons baking powder

½ teaspoon salt

1 teaspoon ground cinnamon

¼ teaspoon ground ginger

¼ teaspoon ground nutmeg

¼ teaspoon ground allspice

¼ cup raisins

1 egg

⅓ cup canned pumpkin

2 tablespoons milk

2 tablespoons solid vegetable shortening, melted

2 tablespoons molasses

2 tablespoons apple butter

Heat oil for deep frying to 350 degrees. Mix flour, baking powder, salt, cinnamon, ginger, nutmeg, and allspice with raisins. Stir in egg, pumpkin, milk, shortening, molasses, and apple butter just until smooth. Drop by teaspoonfuls into deep fat and fry for about 2 minutes, or until crisp and very brown. Drain on paper towels and serve at once.

*Yield:* 2 to 3 dozen

# INDIAN CORNMEAL DUMPLINGS

1½ quarts beef, chicken, or turkey stock

¾ cup flour

1½ teaspoons baking powder

1 teaspoon minced fresh parsley

¼ cup cornmeal

½ teaspoon salt

1 egg, lightly beaten

⅓ cup milk

2 tablespoons solid vegetable shortening, melted

Heat broth to boiling in a deep saucepan. Sift together flour, baking powder, parsley, cornmeal, and salt. Combine egg and milk and add to flour mixture. Stir in melted shortening. Drop by teaspoonfuls into hot stock. Cover lightly and steam for 15 minutes. For light, fluffy dumplings, it is important not to lift lid.

*Yield:* about 24 dumplings

# ◈  CANDIED CARROTS  ◈

Claudia Sanders Dinner House of Shelbyville, Kentucky,
Cookbook *by Cherry Settles, Tommy Settles, and Edward G. Klemm*

*The chefs at the Claudia Sanders Dinner House in Shelbyville,
Kentucky, believe that if rabbits could cook their carrots,
this recipe would be their preference.*

6 or 8 medium-size carrots

½ cup maple syrup

¼ cup water

¾ cup light brown sugar

4 tablespoons (½ stick) butter or margarine, melted

¼ teaspoon ground cinnamon

Boil carrots in salted water for about 25 minutes. Preheat oven to 350 degrees. Peel carrots and cut into small strips. In 1½-quart baking dish, mix maple syrup, water, brown sugar, butter, and cinnamon. Add carrots and toss. Bake for 25 to 30 minutes, or until most of liquid is absorbed.

*Yield:* 6 servings

# BLEU CHEESE-STUFFED POTATOES

6 large baking potatoes
½ cup half-and-half
¼ pound (1 stick) unsalted butter, melted
1 small wedge bleu cheese, crumbled
1 teaspoon white pepper
1½ teaspoons salt

Heat oven to 400 degrees. Bake potatoes for 1 hour, or until tender. Reduce heat to 350 degrees. While hot, halve potatoes and scoop out pulp. Cream pulp, half-and-half, butter, bleu cheese, white pepper, and salt together with electric mixer until well blended. Return pulp to shells and bake for 20 to 25 minutes.

*Yield:* 12 servings

# ASPARAGUS PARMESAN

*Fred and Jenny Wiche*

*Fred Wiche is known to everyone in Kentucky as "the Weekend Gardener." If it weren't for him, I would never be able to grow anything. I featured some of the Wiches' vegetable recipes in* Kentucky Living *and received lots of mail from very happy readers. This is one of my favorites. It is so simple and so elegant. I've served it at many catering events, and guests always rave about it.*

Fresh asparagus
½ cup heavy whipping cream
2 to 3 ounces Parmesan cheese, freshly grated (½ to ¾ cup)

Steam asparagus just until tender. Heat heavy cream with cheese just until cheese melts. Pour over hot, buttered asparagus.

*Yield:* 4 servings

# ZUCCHINI-CHEESE PUDDING

4 small zucchini, thinly sliced

1 tablespoon minced fresh thyme

2 tablespoons butter

4 eggs

1 cup milk

½ cup heavy whipping cream

¾ cup Parmesan cheese

Tabasco to taste

Soda crackers

4 ounces Swiss cheese, grated (1 cup)

Preheat oven to 350 degrees. Sauté zucchini and thyme in butter until zucchini is tender. Beat eggs, milk, heavy cream, Parmesan cheese, and Tabasco until thoroughly mixed. Arrange layer of crackers in well-buttered 2-quart casserole. Top with half each of egg mixture, zucchini, and Swiss cheese. Repeat layers. Let stand for 20 minutes and then bake for 30 to 40 minutes, or until puffy and browned. Serve hot.

*Yield:* 4 to 6 servings

# PINEAPPLE AU GRATIN

1 (20-ounce) can pineapple tidbits with liquid
4 ounces cheddar cheese, grated (1 cup)
¾ cup sugar
3 tablespoons flour
⅓ 15-ounce box (one sleeve) buttery round crackers, crumbled
4 tablespoons (½ stick) butter, melted

Preheat oven to 350 degrees. Drain pineapple, reserving ½ cup liquid. Combine cheese, sugar, and flour and mix until well blended. Add pineapple liquid, then pineapple. Put in greased 2-quart casserole. Pour cracker crumbs over top. Spoon melted butter over cracker crumbs. Bake until bubbly and golden brown (25 to 30 minutes).

*Yield:* 4 servings

# LIMA BEAN CASSEROLE

*Fred And Jenny Wiche*

¼ cup chopped green onion
2 tablespoons butter
1 (2-ounce) jar chopped pimientos
1 cup sour cream
2 cans lima beans, drained, or 2 (14- to 16-ounce) packages frozen
lima beans, cooked and drained
Paprika

Sauté onion in melted butter until soft. Add pimientos, sour cream, and lima beans and simmer just until heated through. Do not allow mixture to boil after sour cream has been added. Sprinkle top with paprika before serving.

*Yield:* 8 servings

# ❧ BRUSSELS SPROUTS ❧
## SUPREME

*Fred and Jenny Wiche*

2 (10-ounce) packages frozen brussels sprouts (or use fresh)

½ cup water

1 cube beef bouillon

¼ cup mayonnaise

1 tablespoon prepared mustard

¼ teaspoon Worcestershire sauce

½ cup sour cream

6 slices bacon, cooked and crumbled

Put brussels sprouts, water, and beef bouillon in 2-quart casserole. Cover. Microwave at High for 13 to 16 minutes, stirring twice. Drain. Stir in mayonnaise, mustard, and Worcestershire sauce. Cover and microwave for 2 or 3 minutes, until hot. Stir once. Stir in sour cream and let stand for 3 minutes. Sprinkle with crumbled bacon.

*Yield:* 4 servings

*Note:* If using regular cooking method on top of stove, boil or steam brussels sprouts until tender.

# RESTAURANT CORN PUDDING

*Brodrick's Tavern*

*Brodrick's Tavern is located fifty-five miles northeast of Lexington in Washington, Kentucky. It is rich in history and has long been one of my favorite places to dine. The food is always wonderful, as well as the service and the atmosphere. If you have a free afternoon, it's worth the drive.*

4 eggs

2 tablespoons self-rising flour

2 tablespoons sugar

2 cans cream-style corn

2 cups whole or 2 percent milk

6 tablespoons (¾ stick) butter, melted

Preheat oven to 350 degrees. Beat eggs. Add flour and sugar. Mix well. Add cream-style corn and milk, mixing well. Pour melted butter into 13 x 9 x 2-inch baking dish. Add corn mixture on top. Bake uncovered for 1 hour.

*Yield:* 10 servings

# EGGPLANT CASSEROLE

Claudia Sanders Dinner House of Shelbyville, Kentucky,
Cookbook *by Cherry Settles, Tommy Settles, and Edward G. Klemm*

*The Claudia Sanders Dinner House in Shelbyville, Kentucky, serves
this eggplant casserole as "Mock Oysters." This dish is excellent. I
can't begin to tell you how many Mother's Day meals I've celebrated
at this great Kentucky restaurant enjoying this favorite.*

2 medium-size eggplants, peeled and cut into small pieces
(about ½-inch cubes; should come to about 4 cups),
soaked about 8 hours in salted water

1 (1-pound) box saltine crackers, broken into coarse crumbs

1 teaspoon salt

½ teaspoon pepper

¼ pound (1 stick) butter

About 1 pint half-and-half

Remove eggplant pieces from the water they have soaked in. In
cooking pot, cover eggplant with fresh, slightly salted water and cook
over medium heat for about 20 minutes, or until eggplant is tender.
Drain in colander.

Preheat oven to 350 degrees. Line bottom of 2-quart casserole with
one-third of the saltine crumbs. Cover with 2 cups of eggplant. Season
with half the salt and pepper. Cut half the butter into small pieces and
sprinkle over top. Cover this with layer of saltine crumbs. Add remaining 2 cups eggplant. Season with the rest of the salt and pepper. Cover
top with remaining saltine crumbs. Cut remaining butter into small
pieces and sprinkle over top of crumbs. Pour in enough half-and-half
to cover. Bake for 1 hour, or until top layer browns.

*Yield:* 8 servings

# BAKED MUSHROOMS

*Ditto House*

*Ditto House, located in West Point, Kentucky,
serves superb breakfasts to its guests.*

1 pound mushrooms, sautéed in butter

2 beef bouillon cubes, dissolved in ½ cup hot water

2 tablespoons flour mixed in 4 tablespoons (½ stick) melted butter

½ cup milk

⅛ teaspoon salt

⅛ teaspoon pepper

½ cup seasoned fine, dried bread crumbs

⅓ cup Parmesan cheese

Preheat oven to 350 degrees. Mix everything except bread crumbs and cheese. Pour into greased 1½-quart casserole. Combine crumbs and cheese and sprinkle on top. Bake for 30 minutes. Let sit for 10 minutes to become firm.

*Yield:* 6 servings

# ❧ COMPANY ONIONS ❧

2 large onions

1 beef bouillon cube

1 cup boiling water

¼ teaspoon thyme

½ teaspoon salt

¼ teaspoon pepper

1 tablespoon butter

½ cup fine fresh bread crumbs

2 tablespoons butter, melted

1⅓ ounces (about ⅓ cup) sharp cheddar cheese, grated

Preheat oven to 400 degrees. Peel and slice each onion into 4 to 6 thick slices. Arrange in 1½-quart baking dish. Dissolve bouillon cube in the boiling water. Add thyme and pour over onions. Sprinkle with salt and pepper and dot with 1 tablespoon butter. Cover and bake for 20 minutes. Toss bread crumbs in 2 tablespoons melted butter and add cheese. Sprinkle over onions and bake uncovered for an additional 10 minutes, or until bread crumbs are browned.

*Yield:* 4 servings

# GREEN PEPPER CASSEROLE

*Fred and Jenny Wiche*

1 cup chopped green peppers
1 cup fine cracker crumbs
4 ounces Velveeta cheese, cubed
4 tablespoons (½ stick) margarine, melted
1 (12-ounce) can evaporated milk

Preheat oven to 350 degrees. Mix all ingredients together and pour into greased casserole. Bake for 20 minutes, or until top is brown.

*Yield:* 3 large or 4 small servings

# VEGETABLE EXTRAVAGANZA

2 cups fine dried Italian bread crumbs
1 (15-ounce) can artichoke hearts, drained and chopped
1 (15-ounce) can French sliced green beans, drained
1½ hard-boiled eggs, chopped
2 ounces Romano or Parmesan cheese, grated (½ cup)
1 cup Italian salad dressing

Preheat oven to 350 degrees. Combine all ingredients, mixing well to moisten bread crumbs. Pour into large greased casserole and bake uncovered for 20 minutes.

*Yield:* 7 to 8 servings

# VIENNA ONIONS

2½ pounds onions, cut into quarters

2 tablespoons sweet sherry

½ cup chopped celery

¼ cup pimientos

1 cup mushrooms

½ teaspoon marjoram

Pinch of thyme

4 tablespoons (½ stick) butter

2 tablespoons flour

1½ cups milk

2 cups fine cracker crumbs

½ pound cheddar cheese, grated (2 cups)

Paprika

Cover onions with water and boil for 5 minutes. Drain. Preheat oven to 325 degrees. Add sherry, celery, pimientos, mushrooms, marjoram, and thyme to onions. Melt butter in second saucepan and slowly blend in flour and milk. Cook until mixture thickens and combine with onions.

Place layers of onion mixture, cracker crumbs, and cheese in 2-quart casserole. Top with paprika and bake for 1 hour.

*Yield:* 8 servings

# CURRIED CATFISH-STUFFED EGGS

1 cup mayonnaise

2 tablespoons cider vinegar

⅓ cup sweet pickle relish

2 tablespoons finely minced onion

¼ teaspoon curry powder

1 teaspoon salt

3 cups cooked catfish (about 3 fillets), flaked

12 hard-boiled eggs

Chopped parsley for garnish

Combine mayonnaise, vinegar, pickle relish, onion, curry powder, and salt. Blend well. Fold in flaked catfish. Cut eggs in half lengthwise and remove yolks. Blend yolks with fish mixture. Spoon fish mixture into egg whites. Garnish with parsley.

*Yield:* 2 dozen stuffed eggs

# ❧ ELEGANT OYSTERS ❧

*This dish is worth the effort. It's truly one of my favorite ways
to serve oysters, but one I save for special occasions.*

1 quart select oysters, liquid reserved

¼ pound (1 stick) unsalted butter

¾ cup flour

1 tablespoon paprika

1 teaspoon salt

½ teaspoon freshly ground pepper

¼ cup finely chopped green onion

¼ cup finely chopped green pepper

½ teaspoon minced garlic

2 teaspoons lemon juice

1 tablespoon Worcestershire sauce

3 tablespoons fine saltine cracker crumbs

Pick over oysters for shells. Heat oysters in own liquid plus enough
water to make 1½ cups liquid.

In a separate saucepan, melt butter, add flour, and cook 5 minutes,
stirring. Add paprika, salt, and pepper and cook slowly, stirring constantly, until dark in color. Do not burn.

Preheat oven to 400 degrees. Add green onion, green pepper, and
garlic to melted butter and cook slowly for 5 more minutes. Remove
from heat and add lemon juice, Worcestershire sauce, and oysters with
liquid, blending well. Pour into buttered 1½-quart casserole and sprinkle
with cracker crumbs. Bake for 30 minutes.

*Yield:* 8 servings

# PEANUT SQUASH CUSTARD

*Fred and Jenny Wiche*

*I know that many people have never heard of peanut squash. If you're lucky enough to find it, try this one. It's so good that it's worth finding the variety and planting your own.*

1 peanut squash

1 tablespoon butter

½ teaspoon baking powder

1 egg

½ teaspoon salt

1 teaspoon ground cinnamon

1 teaspoon ground nutmeg

1 cup light brown sugar

1 tablespoon flour

1 cup milk

Preheat oven to 375 degrees. Cut peanut squash in half. Put halves cut sides down on cookie sheet and bake for 30 minutes. Remove from oven, peel skin off, and mash squash in bowl. Mix together butter, baking powder, egg, salt, cinnamon, nutmeg, brown sugar, flour, and milk. Add to mashed squash. Blend thoroughly. Pour into buttered custard cups. Place filled cups in pan of water. Bake for 45 minutes, or until knife inserted in center comes out clean.

*Yield:* 6 servings

# IMPERIAL SQUASH

2½ pounds yellow squash
1 large onion
4 tablespoons (½ stick) unsalted butter
1 cup light whipping cream
½ pound American cheese, cubed
2 tablespoons cornstarch
½ teaspoon salt
¼ teaspoon pepper
2 (4½-ounce) cans shrimp, drained
20 buttery round crackers, crushed

Preheat oven to 350 degrees. Wash and cut up squash and onion. Boil together in salted water until tender. Drain well and set aside. Combine butter and cream in saucepan. Cook over low heat, stirring constantly. Add cheese, cornstarch, salt, and pepper and allow sauce to thicken. Put squash and onion in 2-quart casserole. Blend in shrimp and cheese sauce and sprinkle with cracker crumbs. Bake uncovered for 20 to 30 minutes.

*Yield:* 8 servings

# BROILED TOMATOES WITH SOUR CREAM

4 tomatoes
Salt and pepper
⅓ cup sour cream
⅓ cup mayonnaise
⅛ teaspoon curry powder

Preheat broiler. Wash and core tomatoes. Do not peel. Cut in half crosswise. Sprinkle with salt and pepper to taste. Blend sour cream, mayonnaise, and curry powder and spread on cut sides of tomatoes. Broil until mixture is bubbly, 5 to 10 minutes.

*Yield:* 4 servings

# GREEN FRIED TOMATOES

*Shady Lane Bed and Breakfast Inn*

*Berea's Shady Lane Bed and Breakfast is so named for all the beautiful trees on the property. This bird lover's paradise offers horseshoes, croquet, and bocci games for patrons and boasts the best green fried tomatoes to be found anywhere.*

6 medium tomatoes (green with only a tinge of pink)

¾ cup cornmeal

¼ cup flour

½ teaspoon salt

¼ teaspoon pepper

½ teaspoon dried oregano

Olive oil for sautéing

Cut tomatoes horizontally into ¼-inch-thick slices, discarding top and bottom slices. Mix cornmeal, flour, salt, pepper, and oregano. Coat tomatoes well with this mixture and let them sit for 15 to 20 minutes. Heat olive oil in skillet and add tomato slices in 1 layer. Lower heat to medium and fry for about 6 minutes, or until golden brown. Drain on paper towels. Repeat with remaining slices.

*Yield:* 8 servings

*Note:* Tomatoes must be green with only a slight tinge of pink or they become soft when fried.

# STEWED TOMATOES

4 to 6 large ripe tomatoes

2 tablespoons sugar

2 tablespoons butter

1 teaspoon salt

½ teaspoon pepper

2 slices dried white bread, coarsely crumbled

Peel tomatoes by boiling for 3 minutes, plunging into ice water (reserving the boiling water), and slipping skins right off. Core and put tomatoes back into reserved water (there should be about 1 cup of water) in saucepan over low heat. Simmer until tender and mash. Add sugar, butter, salt, and pepper and simmer 2 or 3 minutes longer. Remove from heat and add bread crumbs.

*Yield:* 6 to 8 servings

# Main Dishes

# Main Dishes

 My mother-in-law, Flossie Fulkerson Lewis, grew up in Ohio County, Kentucky. I spent many hours listening to her tell me about riding a mule each day to get the mail. My favorite stories were those she told of her mother's kitchen and the meals she shared there with her big family. Many times she sat down to a bountiful table of meat, steaming vegetables, and potatoes of some sort. When she talked of her mother's homemade biscuits, the story would truly make one's mouth water. Many times, though, Flossie would scrunch up her face when she talked about putting butter on the steaming biscuits.

"Sometimes," she would say then, "the cow got into the onions."

Main dishes are as diversified as Kentucky cooking itself. They are also reflective of a cook's own talent and preference. I am as likely to serve a plate of fried chicken with buttermilk biscuits and cream gravy as I am to painstakingly create a beef Wellington fit for the most distinguished connoisseur. The beauty of my appreciation of Kentucky cooking is that, to me, these two dishes are equally fun to prepare and equally delicious. This is key in what I have discovered of main dishes here in the bluegrass state.

In addition to my own collection of main dish favorites, I include here some of the best from noted restaurants throughout the state. Executive Chef Jim Gerhardt of Louisville's Seelbach Hotel, the epitome of fine dining and accommodations in Kentucky, offers us Bluegrass Free-Range Chicken with Three-Herb Pesto—truly a contribution that is an example of the best our state has to offer.

I include my own Favorite Ham with Burnt-Sugar Glaze and Crab-Stuffed Peppers, which are always a big hit at my house. Different regions of Kentucky offer different ways of preparing favorite main dishes, but one thing remains the same: whether it be Country Ham Kentucky Style or Baked Pecan Catfish, Kentucky cooks do it with a style not to be equaled anywhere.

# CHICKEN AND DUMPLINGS

*Cissy Gregg,* Louisville Courier-Journal

*Read this 1946 recipe for everything you ever wanted to know about "sad" dumplings, or read it just for fun. But do read it. It's Cissy Gregg at her best.*

For years it has been a preconceived idea that the real bringer of that "look" in men's eyes was love. Alas, 'tis not true! To prove it to yourself, start up a conversation on love, and if more comes of that than a wan sigh, you have progressed well. But start off with the subject of chicken 'n' dumplin's, and right off you'll be faced with men of strong convictions, ready to go forth to battle for the "kind mother used to make."

All mothers did not make them alike, we have found out. And our dumpling Galahads are willing and eager to go forth in search of a recipe which will produce a facsimile thereof.

Dumplings are not the only item in food we all have definite emotional feelings about. Stories flow freely of happenings where the daughter of a Southern home never could darken its door again because she had gone off and married a man who had to have sugar in his cornbread. Today many of us who have succumbed to this whiff of sweetness in our corn muffins add it behind closed kitchen doors and are driven by conscience to feel as if each pinch was a smudge on our upbringing. We draw another regional line when we think of New Englanders not as people living in the New England states, but those people who, of their own free will, prefer yellow cornmeal to white, coarse, water-ground meal. But with dumplings, the matter changes somewhat. Those who call fat bits of fluff-duff with stewed chicken by the name of dumplings are one kind of people, while those who make sad-flat dumplings to go with their chicken are another kind. The boundaries to hold one kind or the other have nothing to do with geography at all. It's a family affair, and we'll hold on to our type, come what may.

In presenting to you chicken 'n' dumplings, I do not do so with any attempt to change opinion. It is done with the idea that it's time for me to take a stand on dumplings. The matter was brought to my attention by a letter from a fellow Kentuckian who, through trying to do his bit in the war effort, was forced to leave his native haunts and associate with people uncivilized enough to hold the opinion that a flat, rolled-out dumpling was nothing but a noodle, after all. Horrors! What war does bring on people!

It makes small difference the course other cooks take. Those who like "pillows" as dumplings on top of their chicken can have them; but around here, when "Ah-h, my dumpling" is said with endearing tones, you can bet your last dollar the speaker-outer has in mind a thin strip of dumpling that nestles down in the gravy in loving companionship with the pieces of chicken.

Cooks vary in their opinion as to how to make flat dumplings. And all three of these ways leave me without a preference. That you'll have to decide for yourself, and, after all, there's very little to it.

DUMPLING ONE: Make the same kind of pastry you would for pie crust. Use more flour than usual on the board when rolling them out. Roll the dough very, very thin. Cut in strips and drop them into the broth.

DUMPLING TWO: Make a richer-than-average biscuit dough. Go to the half-way place between biscuits and pastry and at that point you'll find the perfect proportion for a dumpling. Cook the same as dumpling No. 1.

DUMPLING THREE: Place in a bowl the amount of flour you would want to make up. Two cups of flour, we'll say. Add salt to taste— we used a good teaspoonful. The chicken has been cooked until it is at the place in doneness that, if it had to take one more simmer, it would suffer a complete breakaway from the bones. At this point, tenderly lift it from the stew pot to a serving bowl and keep hot. If the chicken was fat, with a large serving spoon, stir up the broth, pushing back the fat a little, then dip up a spoonful of the hot liquid and add it to the measured flour in the bowl. Add enough of the chicken broth to make a rather stiff dough. Roll out thin on a well-floured board; cut in strips— I'd say an inch wide—and drop them into the boiling stew. Cover the pot and cook about 10 to 15 minutes. They must be done, though the thickness the dough is rolled will hold the accurate time needed.

When dumplings go in the gravy, usually no other thickening is needed, since the dumplings carry flour with them to insure their cooking as individual strips. But if thickening should be needed, it's O.K. by us. Pour gravy and dumplings over the chicken and watch all make pigs of themselves.

## ∞ BAKED CHICKEN, ∞ BUTTER, AND CREAM

1 frying chicken, cut up

½ cup flour

1½ teaspoons salt

½ teaspoon paprika

¼ teaspoon pepper

1½ cups hot water

4 tablespoons (½ stick) unsalted butter

½ cup nonfat dry milk powder

Preheat oven to 425 degrees. Mix flour, salt, paprika, and pepper. Dip chicken into water and coat with flour mixture. Put skin side up into 13 x 9 x 2-inch baking pan. Dot with butter. Bake for 30 minutes, or until golden brown. Remove from oven and reduce heat to 350 degrees. Pour dry milk around chicken. Cover with aluminum foil. Return to oven and bake for 45 minutes.

*Yield:* 4 servings

# ❧ BLEU CHEESE CHICKEN ❧
## WITH MUSHROOMS

2 teaspoons butter or margarine

1 small clove garlic, minced

2 tablespoons dry white wine

½ pound fresh mushrooms, sliced

1 pound chicken breast fillets, skinned, boned, and cut into strips

2 cups noodles, cooked

½ cup crumbled bleu cheese

2 tablespoons seasoned fresh, coarse bread crumbs

Fresh parsley for garnish

Preheat oven to 350 degrees. Heat butter and garlic in nonstick skillet. Add wine and mushrooms. Sauté quickly over high heat until wine evaporates and mushrooms are lightly browned. Remove mushrooms and add chicken strips. Cook quickly over moderate heat until brown. In greased or nonstick baking dish combine chicken, mushrooms, noodles, and bleu cheese. Sprinkle bread crumbs and parsley over top and bake uncovered for 20 minutes.

*Yield:* 4 servings

# CORNISH GAME HENS

8 (10- to 12-ounce) Cornish game hens
Salt and pepper
⅔ cup Dijon mustard
⅔ cup fresh, coarse white bread crumbs
8 teapoons finely chopped green onion
¼ pound (1 stick) butter
Pineapple juice

Preheat oven to 400 degrees. Rub each bird with salt, pepper, and 2 tablespoons mustard. Sprinkle with bread crumbs. Place each bird in square of foil wrap and fold to center. Add 1 teaspoon green onion, 1 tablespoon butter, and 3 tablespoons pineapple juice to each package. Fold foil tightly and bake for 45 minutes. Open foil and baste hens with their own juice. Continue baking for 15 more minutes without resealing until nicely browned.

*Yield:* 8 servings
*Note:* These birds can be resealed
and taken to a picnic or outdoor meal.

# ⤳ HERB CHICKEN ⤳

*Do you remember the quickest dinner you ever put on the table? I do. It was 1987, and I was frantically trying to complete my first book. My daughter, Noélle, had just spilled a big jar of grape jelly on the floor trying to get my attention when my two sons, Christian and Scott, burst through the front door hollering that they were starving and that they both had ball practice within the hour. Annoyed that my typing had to stop, I opened the pantry and took out two cans of tomato soup and a microwave bag of popcorn. Within five minutes, dinner was on the table. I put Noélle in her high chair, tried not to look at the disbelief on the boys' faces, and said with a smile, "It's healthy!"*
*This quick herb chicken is great and won't cause looks of disbelief.*

2½ to 3 pounds chicken

2 tablespoons olive oil

½ cup sliced mushrooms

2 large onions, chopped

Mixed dried herbs (use your favorite, or choose from basil, thyme, rosemary)

1 tablespoon tomato paste

Cut chicken into serving pieces. Sauté in olive oil until well browned and tender, about 25 minutes. Remove from pan and wrap tightly in foil to keep it warm and moist. In same pan, sauté mushrooms and onions. Add herbs and tomato paste. Cook 6 to 7 minutes longer. Arrange chicken pieces on platter and pour herb mixture over pieces.

*Yield:* 8 servings

# KENTUCKY-STYLE FRIED CHICKEN

3 pounds mixed fryer parts
Vegetable oil or shortening for frying
1½ cups flour
2 teaspoons salt
1 teaspoon pepper
1 teaspoon paprika

Thoroughly wash chicken and pat dry. Heat shortening in heavy skillet until a drop of water placed in the oil will "pop." Combine flour, salt, pepper, and paprika in brown paper bag. Shake each piece of chicken in flour mixture. Put in hot shortening skin side down and fry for 12 to 15 minutes on each side, reducing heat slightly after chicken is turned. Drain well on paper towels.

*Yield:* 6 to 8 servings

# MY FAVORITE MILK GRAVY

3 tablespoons Kentucky Kernel Seasoned Flour, if available
3 tablespoons pan drippings from meat (sausage, bacon, or chicken)
2 cups 2 percent milk
1 teaspoon salt
½ teaspoon pepper

Over medium heat, add flour to hot pan drippings and stir until lightly browned. Add milk, all at once, and stir constantly until thickened and bubbling. Add salt and pepper and serve over potatoes, biscuits, vegetables, or meat.

*Yield:* 4 servings
*Note:* This gravy is also great at breakfast,
served over sliced fresh tomatoes.

# ❧ MY FAMILY'S FAVORITE ❧ CHICKEN AND DUMPLINGS

2 quarts water

1 large chicken, cleaned and cut up (leave skin on)

3 stalks celery, chopped

1 medium onion, chopped

2 tablespoons butter

Salt and pepper

2 cups flour

½ cup solid vegetable shortening

½ teaspoon salt

Cold water

In large Dutch oven bring 2 quarts water containing chicken, celery, onion, and butter to a boil. Cover pot and simmer until chicken is tender. Add salt and pepper to taste. Remove chicken pieces and set aside, covering to keep hot.

In bowl, mix flour, shortening, salt, and cold water—adding a tablespoon of water at a time as you would in making a pie shell—until a stiff dough is formed. Roll out dough on floured surface, again as you would for a pie shell. Cut into strips 2 inches long and as thin as possible.

Bring stock to a boil and stretch strips as you drop them into liquid. Cook uncovered for 10 to 15 minutes.

*Yield:* 4 to 6 servings

# ❧ SMOKED QUAIL ❧

16 quail

Garlic powder

Onion powder

Freshly ground pepper

½ pound (2 sticks) butter or margarine

½ onion, diced

1 (10¾-ounce) can mushroom soup

Curry powder

½ cup red wine

Prepare smoker. Season quail with garlic powder, onion powder, and pepper. Melt butter in skillet and sauté onion. Sauté birds in 1 stick butter in a separate skillet for 8 to 10 minutes. Tear pieces of aluminum foil large enough to put 2 birds in each piece. Lay pairs of birds on foil pieces and cover each pair with about 2 tablespoons butter, 1 tablespoon soup, a pinch of curry powder, and 1 tablespoon sautéed onion. Close foil loosely around birds and put in smoker for 2 hours with red wine in drip pan.

*Yield:* 8 servings

# SUNDAY SUPPER CHICKEN

Salt and freshly ground pepper

2 whole chicken breasts, boned, split, and pounded to flatten

1 (3-ounce) package cream cheese with chives,
cut into quarters and softened

1 large egg, beaten with 1 tablespoon vegetable oil

1½ cups fine, fresh bread crumbs

2 to 4 tablespoons butter

Salt and pepper each open chicken breast. Spread one-fourth of the softened cream cheese on each chicken breast. Fold halves together and secure with toothpicks if they do not hold together. Dip in beaten egg and roll in bread crumbs. These may now be frozen or cooked.
If preparing immediately, fry slowly in butter in nonstick skillet. The chicken cooks quickly because it is thin. Serve immediately.

*Yield:* 4 servings

# CHICKEN PHILIPPE

*Old Talbott Tavern, Betty Kelley, owner*

*It was to Bardstown, Kentucky, that President George Washington directed exiled the future king Louis-Phillippe. The king and his two brothers were anxious to see the western frontier of the New World, which at that time was the area we now know as Kentucky. During their stay at the Talbott Tavern in 1797, a member of the party painted the murals still on the walls of an upstairs room. As legend tells it, Jesse James later used these murals for target practice, which explains the bullet holes in them.*

*Mid-America's oldest restaurant, now in its third century of service, the Talbott Tavern has served such notables as Daniel Boone, Queen Marie of Rumania, General George Patton, and steamboat inventor John Fitch. The* Chicago Tribune *has described the food as "indescribably delicious." I truly consider it to be Kentucky's treasure. The Tavern has been an ongoing food establishment since before Kentucky was a state. Its longevity is a testament to its exceptional service and exquisite cuisine.*

Preheat oven to 325 degrees. Dredge boneless breast of chicken in seasoned flour and brown in skillet with lard. Put in pan coated with butter or margarine to prevent sticking, if necessary. Season with Worcestershire sauce, poultry seasoning, and bay leaf (optional). Bake for about 45 minutes, depending on the size of the chicken breasts. Baste with burgundy wine before serving.

# BLUEGRASS FREE-RANGE CHICKEN

*The Oak Room of the Seelbach Hotel, Jim Gerhardt, executive chef*

*In May 1997, the Seelbach Hotel's executive chef, Jim Gerhardt, prepared his Oakroom's signature Bluegrass Free-Range Chicken with Three-Herb Pesto, Colonel Newsom's Country Ham, and Maker's Mark Bourbon Sauce at the Seventh Annual James Beard Foundation Awards Great Hotel Chefs of America Reception at the New York Marriott Marquis. Chef Gerhardt's Kentucky fine dining menu has won national acclaim as he continues to blend his own tradition of excellence with the great tradition of the Seelbach and Kentucky cuisine.*

*Chef Gerhardt uses tender free-range chickens from the Bell Rouge Farm south of Louisville in preparing this dish. Colonel Bill Newsom is a true Kentucky colonel who "makes hams down around Paducah."*

4 fresh 12- to 14-ounce free-range chicken breasts

4 tablespoons Three-Herb Pesto (recipe follows)

Salt and pepper

2 ounces olive or peanut oil

4 (1-ounce) slices Colonel Bill Newsom's Aged Kentucky Country Ham

12 ounces Maker's Mark Bourbon Sauce (recipe follows)

Preheat oven to 400 degrees. Cut double-lobe chicken breasts in pairs of 2 equal lobes and place on flat surface. Remove tenderloins and set aside. Cover chicken breasts with plastic wrap and pound with meat mallet until chicken is even thickness throughout. On flesh side of chicken, spread 1 tablespoon herb pesto and top with slice of country ham. Place chicken tenderloins in center of breasts. Fold both sides of breasts to or over tenderloins and secure with toothpicks.

When all are complete, heat oil in sauté pan over high heat. Season outside of chicken with salt and pepper and sauté with skin side down until skin is golden brown. Turn chicken over and bake for 15 to 20 minutes, or until chicken reaches 160 degrees internally. Slice each breast into 5 medallions and arrange over bourbon sauce.

*Yield:* 4 servings

# ❦ THREE-HERB PESTO ❦

*The Oak Room of the Seelbach Hotel, Jim Gerhardt, executive chef*

1 bunch of fresh basil

½ bunch of fresh tarragon

½ bunch of fresh cilantro

1 tablespoon chopped garlic

2 ounces toasted pine nuts

1 ounce Parmesan cheese

½ cup extra virgin olive oil

Salt and pepper

Place all ingredients in food processor and chop until minced. Season with salt and pepper to taste. Store in covered container and refrigerate until ready to use.

*Yield:* 4 servings for chicken dish

# MAKER'S MARK
## BOURBON SAUCE

*The Oak Room of the Seelbach Hotel, Jim Gerhard, executive chef*

½ teaspoon olive oil

1 tablespoon shallots

4 ounces Maker's Mark bourbon

12 ounces Oakroom Demi-Glace (recipe follows)

2 ounces gastrique (see note)

½ ounce cornstarch

⅛ cup cold water

Salt and pepper

Heat olive oil in small saucepan over medium heat for 1 minute. Add shallots, cover, and cook over low heat for 2 minutes. Remove pan from heat and add bourbon. Return pan to stove and reduce liquid by 75 percent. (Have pan cover available, because bourbon may flame.)

Add demi-glace and gastrique and bring to a boil. Allow sauce to boil gently for 3 to 5 minutes. Combine cornstarch and water and mix until smooth. Slowly drizzle mixture into sauce while whisking. Bring sauce back to a slow boil and let cook for 2 to 3 minutes. Add salt and pepper to taste.

*Yield:* 4 servings for chicken dish
*Note:* Gastrique is a mixture of 2 tablespoons sugar combined with 2 ounces white vinegar cooked to a medium caramel stage.

# OAKROOM DEMI-GLACE

*The Oak Room of the Seelbach Hotel, Jim Gerhardt, executive chef*

2 pounds veal shank bones, cut into 2-inch pieces

1 gallon plus 1 cup water

3 stalks celery, chopped

6 cloves garlic

3 sprigs thyme

12 black peppercorns

2 carrots, peeled and chopped

1 onion, chopped

2 tablespoons tomato paste

3 bay leaves

2 tablespoons cornstarch mixed with ¼ cup water

Salt and pepper

Heat oven to 400 degrees. Place veal bones in roasting pan and roast until all bones take on rich brown color. Remove bones and place pan on stove on medium heat. Add 1 cup of the water to roasting pan and scrape loose any pieces that may have stuck to pan while roasting bones. Pour water from roasting pan into large stock pot and add veal bones and all remaining ingredients except cornstarch mixture.

Place pot on medium heat, bring to a boil, and allow to boil for 30 minutes. Reduce heat to low and allow to simmer for 8 hours. (You may need to add a little water during this process if stock reduces too quickly.) Strain stock and return liquid to stove over medium heat. Whisk in cornstarch mixture, bring back to a boil for 2 to 3 minutes, and adjust as desired with salt and pepper.

*Yield:* 4 servings for chicken dish

*Note:* 2 (12-ounce) cans of double-strength beef broth thickened with a cornstarch-and-water mixture can be substituted for this demi-glace if needed. At the Seelbach Oakroom in Louisville, Bluegrass Free-Range Chicken with Three-Herb Pesto and Maker's Mark Bourbon Sauce is available nightly à la carte or as part of the Seven-Course Taste of the James Beard House Menu.

# BURGUNDY BEEF PIE

*This is another great comfort meal for a cold winter's night.*

3 pounds lean beef steak, cut into 1-inch cubes

4 tablespoons (½ stick) butter

¼ cup olive oil

3 tablespoons flour

1 can beef consommé

1 cup dry burgundy

1 large onion, thinly sliced

1 pound fresh mushrooms, sliced

¾ cup chopped celery and leaves

1½ teaspoons snipped fresh dill

1 bay leaf

1 tablespoon Worcestershire sauce

Salt

Freshly ground pepper

1 (9-inch) pie shell, unbaked

Melted butter

Brown beef in butter and olive oil in large, heavy skillet. Sprinkle with flour. Stir in consommé, burgundy, onion, mushrooms, celery, dill, bay leaf, Worcestershire sauce, salt, and pepper. Simmer 45 to 50 minutes. Remove bay leaf. Preheat oven to 350 degrees. Pour beef mixture into 2-quart casserole and cover with pie shell rolled into the shape of the casserole. Crimp and seal edges with fork. Brush with melted butter and bake for 30 minutes, or until crust is golden brown.

*Yield:* 6 servings

# HAMBURGER STEW

1 pound ground beef
1 tablespoon minced onion
1 teaspoon minced green pepper
1 tablespoon vegetable oil
1 (16-ounce) can plus 1 (12-ounce) can tomatoes, drained
1 (16-ounce) package frozen mixed vegetables
1 cup cooked wide noodles
½ teaspoon salt

Sauté beef, onion, and green pepper in oil in heavy skillet over medium heat until browned. Add tomatoes, vegetables, noodles, and salt. Mix well and cook 20 minutes longer.

*Yield:* 8 servings

# ❧ MEAT LOAF ❧

*Throughout the years I've heard so many negative comments about meat loaf, and I've never understood it. My mother always made a great meat loaf, and no one was ever disappointed when they knew that was what she was serving. I also love leftovers as a sandwich with Dijon-style mustard the next day. This is my mother's recipe.*

2 slices bread

Enough milk to saturate bread

2 pounds ground chuck

2 eggs, lightly beaten

2 heaping tablespoons flour

1 medium onion, chopped

1 green pepper, chopped

1⅓ cups ketchup

½ teaspoon garlic powder

1 teaspoon salt

½ teaspoon pepper

2 tablespoons water

Preheat oven to 350 degrees. Crumble bread in large bowl. Pour milk over top and allow to saturate completely. Add ground chuck, eggs, flour, onion, green pepper, 1 cup of the ketchup, garlic powder, salt, and pepper and mix together.

Form 2 loaves in 1 large baking dish. Mix the remaining ⅓ cup ketchup with 2 tablespoons water and pour around loaves in baking dish. Rub tops of loaves with additional ketchup and bake, covered tightly with foil, for 45 minutes. Uncover and bake an additional 15 minutes.

*Yield:* 8 to 10 servings

# COUNTRY FRIED STEAK

*If you're looking for a great Kentucky country fried steak, t*
*is as good as it gets.*

½ cup flour

½ teaspoon salt

¾ teaspoon pepper

1½ teaspoons paprika

1 (1½-pound) boneless round steak, about ¾ inch thick,
trimmed of excess fat

3 tablespoons bacon or ham fat

1½ cups milk

Salt and pepper

Cayenne

Mix flour, salt, pepper, and paprika in small bowl. Set aside 3 tablespoons of this mixture for gravy. Rub half the remaining seasoned flour into one side of steak. Place steak between two sheets of waxed paper and pound with flat side of meat mallet. Turn steak over, rub in the remaining half of the flour mixture, and repeat pounding process. Cut meat into serving pieces.

Heat fat over high heat in large heavy skillet. Brown meat about 2 minutes on each side over high heat. Lower heat, cover, and simmer meat for 45 minutes, until very tender, turning halfway through cooking time. Remove meat from skillet and cover with aluminum foil to keep warm.

Stir reserved flour mix into pan drippings. As soon as flour begins to brown, slowly add milk, stirring constantly. Cook over medium heat and stir until gravy is smooth and thickened. Add salt, pepper, and cayenne to taste. Pour over steaks and serve.

*Yield:* 4 servings

# LIVER AND ONIONS

2 large Vidalia onions
Bacon grease for sautéing
1 pound calves' liver, thinly sliced
Flour for dredging
Salt and pepper

Slice onions very thin and sauté in bacon grease in cast-iron skillet until golden color. Remove from skillet. Lightly dredge liver slices in flour, put in same skillet, and brown on both sides over medium heat. Reduce heat and add onion slices. Cover and simmer for 10 to 12 minutes. Salt and pepper to taste.

*Yield:* 4 servings

# SWISS STEAK

*Loretto Motherhouse*

*The Sisters of Loretto have lived in Nerinx, Kentucky, since 1824, working, worshipping, and welcoming all to their motherhouse.*

¼ cup flour
¼ teaspoon salt
½ teaspoon pepper
1 pound (about 6 pieces) beef steak, preferably bottom round
1 tablespoon vegetable oil
½ large onion, sliced
1 cup tomatoes, cored and chopped
¼ cup water
½ green pepper, sliced

Combine flour, salt, and pepper. Coat steaks in flour mixture. Heat oil in skillet. Brown steaks well on both sides. Steam onion and tomatoes in water for 3 minutes. Add to browned steak. Cover and simmer 1½ hours. Add green pepper slices, cover, and simmer ½ hour more, or until meat and peppers are tender.

*Yield:* 6 servings

## ❧ KENTUCKY ❧ BEEF WELLINGTON

*Maker's Mark Distillery, from* That Special Touch *by Sandra Davis*

1 (7-pound) beef tenderloin, trimmed

1 (8-ounce) package liverwurst spread

1 cup chopped fresh mushrooms

3 tablespoons Maker's Mark bourbon

1 (16-ounce) package frozen puff pastry, thawed

1 egg yolk

1 tablespoon whole or 2 percent milk

Parsley for garnish

Preheat oven to 425 degrees. Put tenderloin on rack in shallow roasting pan. Bake uncovered for 25 to 30 minutes. Remove from oven and let stand 30 minutes. Mix liverwurst spread, mushrooms, and bourbon. Set aside.

Roll pastry to 14 x 20-inch rectangle on lightly floured surface. Spread ⅓ of liverwurst mixture over top of beef and then place beef, top side down, in middle of pastry. Spread remaining liverwurst mixture over bottom and sides of beef. Bring sides of pastry up and overlap to form a seam, trimming off excess pastry. Seal pastry at all edges. Invert to roast.

Combine egg yolk and milk; brush evenly over pastry. I make decorative designs from leftover pastry. Brush with egg mixture. Bake uncovered in lightly greased 13 x 9 x 2-inch pan for 30 to 40 minutes. Let stand 15 minutes before slicing. Garnish with parsley.

*Yield:* 16 servings

# SHEPHERD'S PIE

1½ pounds ground chuck

2 medium onions, chopped fine

3 tablespoons butter or margarine

1 teaspoon Worcestershire sauce

Salt and freshly ground pepper

2 cups beef stock

2 eggs, separated

½ cup heavy whipping cream

¼ pound (1 stick) butter

¼ teaspoon garlic powder

8 potatoes, peeled, cooked, and mashed

Parmesan cheese

Preheat oven to 350 degrees. Brown meat in skillet and drain. Sauté onions in butter in another skillet until golden in color. Combine meat with onions, Worcestershire sauce, salt, and pepper. Add small amount of beef stock, cover, and cook over low heat for 15 minutes.

Beat egg yolks until light in color. Beat egg whites until stiff. Beat yolks, cream, butter, and garlic powder into potatoes. Gently fold beaten egg whites into potatoes. Pour meat mixture into large glass pie plate and spread potato mixture over top. Sprinkle with Parmesan cheese. Bake until puffed and brown, about 40 to 45 minutes.

*Yield:* 6 servings

# VEAL PARMESAN

1 pound boneless veal, cut into thin slices

⅓ cup olive oil

½ pound fresh mushrooms, sliced

1 clove garlic, chopped

¼ cup dry sherry

½ teaspoon salt

¼ teaspoon freshly ground pepper

½ teaspoon rosemary

1 cup Parmesan cheese

Preheat oven to 350 degrees. Brown meat in oil in skillet. Transfer to greased 1-quart casserole. Sauté mushrooms and garlic in remaining oil for 3 to 5 minutes. Pour over meat. Deglaze skillet with sherry and salt, pepper, and rosemary and bring to a boil. Pour over casserole. Sprinkle with Parmesan cheese and bake uncovered for 45 minutes.

*Yield:* 6 servings

# ∽ COUNTRY HAM ∽ KENTUCKY STYLE

Claudia Sanders Dinner House of Shelbyville, Kentucky,
Cookbook *by Cherry Settles, Tommy Settles, and Edward G. Klemm*

*When it came to country ham and giving directions for the novice as
well as the experienced cook, I had many experts from Kentucky to
choose from. I decided to give you the simple, detailed instructions
from the Claudia Sanders Dinner House in Shelbyville. For thirty
years it has served some of the best Kentucky cuisine you'll find in
our state. I have enjoyed so many Mother's Day meals there, and its
country ham has always been a favorite of mine. No Kentucky
cookbook would be complete without instructions that allow each of
us to serve a country ham Kentucky style and do it with pride.*

Carefully clean the ham, by scrubbing with either a stiff brush or a
coarse cloth, before cooking. Cut off the hock, which can be used for
seasoning with beans, etc. Soak the ham for 12 to 14 hours in cold
water. Do not cook your ham in this soaking water.

Your ham is now ready for cooking. There are several ways of cooking a country ham. You can either bake it in a large roasting pan or boil
it submerged in a large container. If you will carefully follow the instructions, either method will prove satisfactory. Regardless of which
process you use, please remember to cook your ham very slowly. This
prevents excessive shrinkage and also allows the ham to absorb desirable moisture.

**To Bake the Ham**
This method is preferred by many people as it eliminates the use of
a large container.

1. Use a roasting pan large enough to hold the ham.

2. Place a piece of heavy-duty aluminum foil, large enough to wrap
the ham, in the bottom of the roasting pan. Place the ham on the foil
and pour over it 1 quart of water, ½ cup of wine vinegar, and 2 cups of

brown sugar. Fold the foil over the top of the ham and put the top on the roaster.

3. Place in a very slow oven: 275 to 300 degrees.

4. Your cooking time will average from 4 to 6 hours, depending on the size of the ham.

5. Your ham is done when:

    A. it feels tender when tested with a fork,

    B. the large bone on the butt end protrudes,

    C. the rind peels off easily.

6. The ham should be allowed to cool in the pan with wrapping intact.

7. When ham is cool, carefully peel off the rind and trim off any excess fat.

8. To glaze the ham, see below.

**To Boil or Simmer the Ham**

1. Place the ham in a large container. Completely cover it with fresh cold water. Put on the stove and bring to a boil—then allow to slowly simmer until the ham is tender, or until the large bone in the butt end of the ham becomes loose and protrudes. Your cooking time will average about 25 minutes to the pound. Add water, if necessary, to keep the ham completely covered.

2. Allow the ham to cool in the cooking water. This causes the ham to retain desirable moisture.

3. When the ham has cooled, carefully remove the rind and trim any excess fat.

4. To glaze the ham, see below.

**To Glaze the Ham**

Make a mix of fine bread crumbs or coarse, water-ground cornmeal and brown sugar, half and half. Add enough port wine or fruit juice so it will spread over the ham. Place the ham back in the oven and brown at 400 degrees until the sugar is bubbly and a crust forms. Decorate to taste.

    *OR*

Mix 1 cup of brown sugar with 3 tablespoons of port wine or fruit juice and spread this mixture over the ham. Decorate to your own taste. Place the ham in the oven and bake at 375 to 400 degrees for 15 to 20 minutes.

### To Carve the Ham

Ham should be cut and served only after it has cooled to room temperature, never while it is hot.

1. Place ham with fat side up.

2. Start slicing at the small or hock end, cutting at a 45-degree angle.

3. Always cut slices as thin as possible.

4. Save all fat and scraps; then when you have used all the slices, the scraps and fat can be put through a food chopper together for mixing as sandwich spread or with scrambled eggs, etc.

### Fried Country Ham

1. Trim off rind and dark, hard edge of 1 (¼-inch) slice of Claudia Sanders Kentucky Country Ham.

2. Trim most of fat from ham and render this fat in a skillet.

3. After all the grease has been cooked out of the fat, remove the fat from the skillet.

4. Put the slice of ham in the medium-hot skillet and brown one side. (Caution: Cook slowly. Do not let skillet become too hot.)

5. Turn the ham and brown the other side.

6. Repeat until the ham is cooked to your taste. (Caution: If cooked too long, the ham will become hard and dry.)

Should the ham be too salty for your taste, you can soak it in water or in milk and sweet syrup for 15 to 30 minutes before cooking.

# HAM AND POTATO CROQUETTES

*This is a favorite of mine on nights
when there isn't much time to prepare dinner.
Add a green salad and bread and you have a great meal.*

3 potatoes

½ cup minced leftover ham

1 egg

Dash of ground nutmeg

Salt and pepper

3 tablespoons cooking oil

3 tablespoons margarine

Peel, grate, and rinse potatoes. Mix with ham and egg. Season with nutmeg, and salt and pepper to taste. Mix well. Shape into small croquettes. Heat oil and margarine in skillet and sauté croquettes until golden brown, turning often. Put on hot serving dish and keep warm.

*Yield:* 12 to 15 croquettes

# SCALLOPED HAM AND POTATOES

*Lorene Fulkerson*

*Scalloped ham and potatoes is a dish I've enjoyed for as long as I can remember. It's still a great one-dish meal on busy days and a great comfort food in cold weather. Of all the recipes for this old favorite, Lorene Fulkerson's is best.*

4 tablespoons (½ stick) margarine

¼ cup flour

2 cups skim milk

1 teaspoon salt

½ teaspoon pepper

6 medium potatoes, peeled and thinly sliced

2 small onions, chopped

2 cups chopped cooked ham

½ pound Velveeta cheese, grated (2 cups)

Preheat oven to 350 degrees. Make white sauce by melting margarine in saucepan over low heat and adding flour, stirring well until smooth. Cook 1 minute, stirring constantly. Add milk gradually. Cook over medium heat, stirring constantly, until mixture is thick and bubbly. Add salt and pepper.

Pour ¼ cup white sauce in 12 x 8 x 2-inch or 13 x 9 x 2-inch greased baking dish. Layer potatoes, onions, ham, remaining white sauce, and cheese. Cover and bake for 1 hour. Uncover and bake 5 minutes more.

*Yield:* 8 servings

# ❦ MY FAVORITE HAM ❦ WITH BURNT-SUGAR GLAZE

1 (8- to 10-pound) boned ham

Whole cloves

1 cup bourbon

1 cup light brown sugar

1 teaspoon grated orange peel

1 cup crushed pineapple

1 tablespoon prepared mustard

Preheat oven to 350 degrees. Cook ham in roasting pan according to package directions. Take ham out 90 minutes before time is up.

Score ham with a lattice design through layer of fat and stud with cloves. Mix remaining ingredients together and pour over ham, basting every 30 minutes during the next 90 minutes of cooking time. Reduce heat to 300 degrees and bake for about 30 more minutes, basting every 15 minutes until the ham feels tender when pierced with a fork. Total cooking time is 2 to 2½ hours, based on 15 minutes per pound.

*Yield:* 18 to 20 servings

# PORK CHOPS WITH ORANGE GLAZE

4 (¾-inch) pork chops

Salt and pepper

Flour for dredging

1 tablespoon vegetable oil

½ cup orange juice

2 tablespoons orange marmalade

2 tablespoons light brown sugar

1 tablespoon cider vinegar

Sprinkle pork chops lightly with salt and pepper and dredge in flour. Heat oil in heavy skillet and brown chops on both sides. Combine orange juice, orange marmalade, brown sugar, and vinegar, mixing well. Pour over pork chops. Reduce heat, cover, and simmer 40 to 45 minutes.

*Yield:* 4 servings

# ❧ RED BEANS AND RICE ❧

1 pound dried red beans

2 quarts water

¾ pound ham hocks

3 cups chopped onion

1 bunch green onions with tops, chopped

1 cup chopped green pepper

2 large cloves garlic, crushed

¾ tablespoon chopped parsley

1 tablespoon salt

¾ teaspoon crushed red pepper

1 teaspoon black pepper

¼ teaspoon oregano

1 large bay leaf

4 to 5 dashes of Tabasco

1 tablespoon Worcestershire sauce

Cooked rice

Cover beans with water and soak about 8 hours. Drain and bring to boil in 2 quarts of water. Lower heat and continue cooking for 45 minutes. Add remaining ingredients and cook slowly for 3 hours, stirring occasionally. Serve over cooked rice.

*Yield:* 6 servings

# FINCHVILLE COUNTRY HAM FRITTATA

*Lynn's Paradise Café*

*Lynn's Paradise Café, Louisville, Kentucky, featured in* Food and Wine *is owned and operated by Lynn Winter and serves some of the best food in all of Kentucky. Everything I order there is always great. The decor is unique, the service always friendly, and Lynn Winter always has a big smile on her face.*

Vegetable oil for sautéing

1 small green bell pepper, chopped

1 small red bell pepper, chopped

1 small white onion, finely chopped

2 cups whole eggs

2 cups heavy whipping cream

1½ cups diced Finchville or other country ham

2 cups grated cheddar cheese

1 cup grated Jack or Mozzarella cheese

1 cup fresh spinach, cut into ribbons

2 cups cooked, diced potatoes

½ teaspoon fresh dill weed

½ teaspoon dried thyme

½ teaspoon dried oregano

½ teaspoon garlic powder

Hollandaise Sauce (optional, recipe follows)

Chopped fresh parsley for garnish

Snipped fresh chives for garnish

Preheat oven to 350 degrees. Heat vegetable oil in skillet. Add green and red peppers and onion and sauté until just cooked. Set aside.

In large mixing bowl, whisk eggs and cream. Stir in ham and cheeses. Drain liquid from vegetables, combine with spinach and potatoes, and add them to egg mixture. Stir gently. Stir in seasonings. Pour into greased 12 x 9-inch baking dish, leaving at least one-fourth to one-half inch for frittata to rise. Cover and bake for 45 to 55 minutes. Shake pan to determine that frittata is firm in center and cooked through. Uncover and bake for 10 more minutes to allow top to brown. Let cool in pan for 10 to 15 minutes.

Slice into squares and serve topped with Hollandaise Sauce if desired. Garnish with chopped fresh parsley and chives.

*Yield:* 8 to 10 servings

## ⊗ HOLLANDAISE SAUCE ⊗

*This is a good sauce to accompany Lynn's Frittata.*

3 egg yolks
1½ tablespoons fresh lemon juice
Pinch of salt
½ pound (2 sticks) unsalted butter, melted
White pepper

Whisk egg yolks and 1 tablespoon of the lemon juice together in top of double boiler. Add pinch of salt and whisk until sauce is thick and creamy. Set double boiler over low heat and continue whisking. Whisk until egg mixture thickens enough that the wires of the whisk make indentations in sauce. Remove from heat. Drizzle melted butter while whisking. Use all the butter except the milky substance. This can be spooned out. Add white pepper to taste. Add remaining lemon juice.

*Yield:* 1½ cups

# SAUSAGE AND EGG CASSEROLE

*Shady Lane Bed and Breakfast*

*Clarine Webber, the owner of Shady Lane Bed and Breakfast in Berea, Kentucky, offers her guests a printed handout titled "Why Don't We?" One of these handouts told of a mother who, concerned that her Thanksgiving meant only turkey, pumpkin pie, and football, decided to begin a new family tradition. She took an empty oatmeal box, cut a slit in it, and covered it with pretty paper. It became her family's "Thank you, God" box. Throughout the year, family members put thank you notes for all sorts of things and a small donation for each in the pretty box. The next Thanksgiving, they opened the box, read the notes about what everyone was grateful for throughout the year, and gave the donations to a worthy cause. What a lovely Thanksgiving gesture —and so meaningful for kids.*

*I love this recipe as a busy holiday morning breakfast dish. I mix the night before and bake the following morning.*

1 pound bulk pork sausage

6 eggs

2 cups milk

1 teaspoon salt

1 teaspoon dry mustard

6 slices white bread, cut into ½-inch cubes

4 ounces cheddar cheese, grated (1 cup)

¼ cup chopped mushrooms (optional)

Brown and crumble sausage in skillet; drain and set aside. In large bowl, beat eggs; add milk, salt, and mustard. Stir in bread pieces, cheddar cheese, sausage, and mushrooms, if desired. Pour into greased 13 x 9 x 2-inch baking dish. Cover and refrigerate overnight, if desired (remove 30 minutes before baking), or bake immediately. Preheat oven to

350 degrees. Bake uncovered for 40 minutes, or until knife inserted comes out clean.

Yield: 8 to 10 servings
Note: Whole wheat or sourdough bread
are good substitutes for white bread.


## ∞ COWBOY BREAKFAST ∞ CASSEROLE

*Every time I serve this dish, people insist on the recipe. It's quite a hit at potlucks, brunches, and of course breakfast on a very special morning.*

1 pound pork sausage
⅓ pound chopped fresh mushrooms
1 medium onion, chopped
10 eggs
4 tablespoons sour cream
Salt and pepper
8 tablespoons salsa
½ pound cheddar cheese, grated (2 cups)
½ pound Monterey Jack cheese, grated (2 cups)
½ pound Mexican Velveeta cheese, grated (2 cups)

Sauté sausage, mushrooms, and onion in large skillet until done. Drain and set aside. Preheat oven to 400 degrees.

Combine eggs and sour cream and season with salt and pepper. Whip egg mixture for 1 minute in blender and pour into 13 x 9 x 2-inch baking dish. Bake until softly set, 6 to 8 minutes.

Spoon salsa evenly over top of eggs. Spread sausage mixture over top. Sprinkle with combined cheeses and refrigerate until 30 minutes before serving time. Then bake in 325-degree oven for 30 minutes.

Yield: 10 servings

# ⚮ SMOKED SAUSAGE STEW ⚮

1 (14- to 17-ounce) can English peas with liquid

1¼ pounds smoked sausage, cut into ½-inch slices

1 (16-ounce) can onion soup, undiluted

1 (16-ounce) can whole tomatoes with liquid

2 cups peeled, cubed potatoes

½ teaspoon Worcestershire sauce

¼ cup flour

Drain peas, reserving ½ cup liquid. Cook sausage in Dutch oven until browned; drain. Add peas, onion soup, tomatoes with liquid, potatoes, and Worcestershire sauce. Bring mixture to a boil; reduce heat and simmer uncovered for 20 minutes, or until potatoes are tender.

Stir reserved pea liquid into flour; gradually add to sausage mixture. Cook over medium heat, stirring constantly, until thickened and bubbly.

*Yield:* 8 servings

# BAKED CHILI RELLENOS

*I learned to love this dish during my restaurant critic days
in the Dallas-Fort Worth area. There are many versions,
but this remains my favorite.*

1½ pounds sausage

1 medium onion, chopped

2 (7-ounce) cans green chilies, drained and chopped

1 pound Colby or cheddar cheese, grated (4 cups)

½ pound Monterey Jack cheese, grated (2 cups)

4 eggs

2 tablespoons flour

½ teaspoon salt

1 (13-ounce) can evaporated milk

Preheat oven to 350 degrees. Brown sausage and onion and drain.
Layer sausage and onion, chilies, and Colby cheese in 2-quart casserole.
Mix together Monterey Jack cheese, eggs, flour, salt, and evaporated
milk and pour over sausage, chilies, and Colby cheese. Bake for 45
minutes.

*Yield:* 6 servings

# BAKED FISH FOR COMPANY

1½ cups mayonnaise

1 tablespoon creole mustard

2 teaspoons lemon juice

1 tablespoon Tabasco

1 tablespoon Worcestershire sauce

2 teaspoons garlic powder

¾ teaspoon curry powder

8 of your favorite fish fillets

Buttery round crackers, crumbled

Preheat oven to 400 degrees. Mix mayonnaise, mustard, lemon juice, Tabasco, Worcestershire sauce, garlic powder, and curry powder well and spread over fish fillets. Sprinkle with crumbled crackers and bake uncovered for 20 to 25 minutes. Fish is done when it flakes easily.

*Yield:* 8 servings

# BAKED PECAN CATFISH

*I've loved catfish for as long as I can remember. My uncle Ed used to catch them from his boat and begin frying them in the morning. I was the only kid I knew who loved fresh catfish at 10 in the morning. This recipe will be a hit with catfish lovers.*

1 egg, beaten

1 cup buttermilk

1 cup flour

2 teaspoons salt

1 tablespoon paprika

¼ teaspoon pepper

1 cup ground pecans

¼ cup sesame seeds

¼ pound (1 stick) margarine, melted

2 pounds catfish

¼ cup pecan halves

Lemon wedges for garnish

Fresh parsley for garnish

Preheat oven to 350 degrees. Combine egg with buttermilk. Sift together flour, salt, paprika, and pepper. Add ground pecans and sesame seeds. Add flour mixture to buttermilk and blend well. Pour margarine into 13 x 9 x 2-inch baking dish. Coat fish with batter. Put in baking dish and put pecan halves on top of fish. Bake for 30 minutes, or until fish is golden brown and flakes easily. Garnish with lemon wedges and parsley.

*Yield:* 8 servings

# CRAB-STUFFED PEPPERS

6 green peppers

1 cup light cream

4 tablespoons (½ stick) butter

¼ teaspoon ground nutmeg

2 tablespoons cornstarch

¼ cup dry white wine

1 tablespoon lemon juice

¼ teaspoon Worcestershire sauce

1 teaspoon salt

2 cups cooked crabmeat

1 cup cooked rice

Paprika

Cut tops off peppers and remove seeds. Cook peppers in boiling water for 5 minutes and drain. Preheat oven to 350 degrees. Scald cream (heat it till it coats a spoon) and add butter and nutmeg. Mix cornstarch, wine, lemon juice, Worcestershire sauce, and salt. Add to cream mixture. Cook until thickened, stirring constantly. Combine with crabmeat and rice and spoon into peppers. Sprinkle with paprika. Put in greased baking dish and bake for 25 minutes.

*Yield:* 6 servings

# ❦ VENISON ❦
# SPAGHETTI SAUCE

1 tablespoon vegetable oil

1 pound ground venison

1 medium onion, thinly sliced

¼ cup chopped green pepper

3 cloves garlic, minced

1 (28-ounce) can Italian pear tomatoes

1 (6-ounce) can tomato paste

¼ cup chopped parsley

1 tablespoon sugar

1½ teaspoons oregano

½ teaspoon aniseed

1 teaspoon salt

2 teaspoons dried basil

½ teaspoon freshly ground pepper

1 cup dry red wine

Heat vegetable oil in heavy saucepan and add venison, onion, green pepper, and garlic. Cook until onion slices are tender and meat loses its pink color. Mash tomatoes with fork and add to meat mixture. Cover and cook for about 5 minutes. Uncover and stir in tomato paste, parsley, sugar, oregano, aniseed, salt, basil, pepper, and wine. Bring to a boil. Reduce heat, cover, and simmer 1½ to 2 hours, or until meat is very tender. Add water if sauce becomes too thick before meat is tender. Serve over cooked spaghetti. Sprinkle with Parmesan cheese, if desired.

*Yield:* 5 cups

# VENISON STIR-FRY

1 pound venison

½ cup soy sauce

2 tablespoons red wine vinegar

2 tablespoons red wine

3 tablespoons vegetable oil

¼ cup thinly sliced green onion

2 cloves garlic, minced

1½ teaspoons grated fresh ginger root

3 carrots, peeled and cut into thin strips

3 stalks celery, cut into thin strips

1 green pepper, thinly sliced

2 small zucchini, thinly sliced

1 medium tomato, cut into wedges

Salt and pepper

Put venison in freezer until semisolid and easy to slice. Cut into strips about ½ inch wide by 3 inches long and put in glass dish. Cover with soy sauce, wine vinegar, and wine. Cover tightly and marinate for 24 hours, turning several times. Remove venison from marinade and drain on paper towel. Set marinade aside for later use.

In large wok, heat oil until very hot. Add venison and stir-fry very quickly. Push meat to sides and add green onion, garlic, and ginger root. Stir-fry quickly and add carrots, celery, green pepper, and zucchini, in that order, stir-frying after each addition. Add tomatoes and 3 to 4 tablespoons of leftover marinade. Simmer 5 minutes longer. Season with salt and pepper to taste. Serve over cooked rice.

*Yield:* 4 to 6 servings

# ⮞ LEG OF LAMB ⮜
## WITH MINT SAUCE

1 (5- to 6-pound) leg of lamb

2 tablespoons butter, melted

1 tablespoon oil

1 tablespoon salt

1 cup water

½ cup sugar

1 teaspoon freshly ground pepper

¾ cup white vinegar

1 teaspoon Worcestershire sauce

2 tablespoons strained bottled mint sauce

Preheat oven to 450 degrees. Rinse meat and dry with paper towel. Combine melted butter and oil and brush lamb with mixture. Put in roasting pan and roast for 20 to 25 minutes, turning often, until browned on all sides. Remove pan from oven and reduce heat to 325 degrees. Place meat thermometer in thickest part of meat and sprinkle the salt in sides of pan. Add the water and stir. Sprinkle sugar, pepper, and vinegar over meat and baste well. Return to oven and roast for 90 minutes, or until thermometer reaches 160 degrees. Baste often during cooking.

When lamb is done, remove from pan to large platter. Cover with foil to keep hot. Skim all fat from liquid remaining in pan. Add Worcestershire sauce and mint sauce to fat. Reheat and serve with lamb. Sauce will be very thin.

*Yield:* 8 servings

# LAYERED SAUERKRAUT
# AND NEFFLES

*Two of my favorite people during my childhood were my great aunts
Frank and Matt. Their given names were Francis and Martha. They were
as different and as colorful as two people can be. Aunt Frank was forever
young in mind and spirit and loved to be around children, always
hanging onto their every word and smiling. Aunt Matt, on the other
hand, worried about everything and made her presence known by her
stern looks to anyone shorter than she was. We were always on our best
behavior, though, when she visited, because we knew she would make this
favorite dish that my mother still makes upon request today. This is my
mother's version. "Neffles" are tiny dumplings.*

2 cups flour

1 teaspoon salt

1 teaspoon baking powder

2 tablespoons oil or solid vegetable shortening, melted

1 egg, lightly beaten

¾ cup cold water

2 quarts boiling water

4 slices bacon

2 large onions, thinly sliced

1 (32-ounce) bag fresh sauerkraut, drained

Salt and pepper

Combine flour, salt, and baking powder. Add oil, egg, and cold
water. Mix well. Drop by teaspoonfuls into boiling water. Cook uncovered approximately 15 minutes over medium heat. Drain and set aside.

Fry bacon in heavy skillet until crisp. Remove, drain, and, when cooled,
crumble. Sauté onions in bacon fat until clear. In another saucepan heat
sauerkraut thoroughly. In 13 x 9 x 2-inch glass baking dish, layer half the
sauerkraut, half the dumplings, half the crumbled bacon, and half the
onions. Repeat layers, salt and pepper to taste, and serve immediately.

*Yield:* 8 servings

# Lunch and Teatime Favorites

# Lunch and Teatime Favorites

 Many years ago, David Hicks of Bardstown, Kentucky, traveling quite a distance, went to visit his Grandma Brown. He was three and a half and had never tasted crunchy peanut butter; his mother always bought the creamy type. His grandmother recalls that, upon his arrival, she fixed lunch and served it to him, only to be told, "I don't eat peanut butter with bones in it."

As I grow older, I appreciate more and more the occasion of a lunch shared with special friends in my home. I find myself putting as much energy and emphasis on preparing lunch as I do more lavish meals. To me, it is a time to laugh and talk in a light atmosphere, and I want the meal to reflect the pleasure of this chance to spend much-needed time with friends. I enjoy preparing a good mushroom soup and a loaf of crusty bread as much as I love to prepare fajitas on the grill and set out small dishes of sour cream, pico de gallo, and guacamole accompaniments. I prefer lunch to be light, even though a more hearty meal can help offset a dinner that will be spent in a hurry.

I have wonderful memories of lunches during my childhood. My grandmother, Loraine Beasy, would take me shopping almost every

Saturday in downtown Louisville. We would spend hours trying on shoes and hats at Stewart's and Byck's. We would usually go to the Colonnade for lunch, and it was there that I came to appreciate Benedictine spread and ribbon sandwich varieties. I remember wearing white gloves and watching my grandmother, who had impeccable taste, appreciate foods served somewhere other than her own wonderful kitchen.

A tea can be used as an opportunity to try different spreads and finger sandwiches. A delicious brunch idea is the Cheese-Stuffed Toast from the Jailer's Inn Bed and Breakfast, which can be assembled the night before and baked at the appropriate time. The Russian Tea Cakes go well on afternoon occasions, and the Country Ham Slivers on Raspberry-Lemon Scones are impressive when a heartier dish is desired.

Whenever I watch my daughter sit pouring "tea" in her miniature silver tea set, I am reminded of cream cheese sandwiches on toast, of white gloves and hats, and of how I treasure today spending moments like these with those close to me. A special lunch or a tea with friends can be a gift to yourself and a memory worth making--one worthy of the most exciting dishes you can offer.

# CHORIZO WEDGES WITH CHEESE

8 ounces chorizo

4 ounces mild cheddar cheese, grated (1 cup)

4 ounces Monterey Jack cheese, grated (1 cup)

3 (10-inch) flour tortillas

Red or green salsa

Remove and discard casing from sausage. Heat medium skillet over high heat until hot. Reduce heat to medium and crumble chorizo into skillet. Brown for 6 to 8 minutes, stirring to separate meat. Remove with slotted spoon and drain. Preheat oven to 450 degrees. Mix cheeses. Put tortillas on baking sheets. Divide chorizo evenly among tortillas and sprinkle cheese mixture on top. Bake for 8 to 10 minutes, until edges are crisp and cheese is bubbly and melted. Transfer to serving plates and cut each tortilla into 6 wedges. Sprinkle salsa over top.

*Yield:* 4 servings

# CRAB MOUSSE

2 envelopes (2 tablespoons) unflavored gelatin

½ cup water

1 pound cooked crabmeat

1 hard-boiled egg

1 cup mayonnaise

2 tablespoons white distilled vinegar

1 tablespoon plus 1 teaspoon chopped fresh parsley

2 tablespoons sweet pickle relish, drained

1 cup heavy cream, whipped

Red lettuce

Combine gelatin and water in saucepan. Cook over medium heat until gelatin dissolves. Remove from heat and set aside. Finely chop crabmeat and egg; mix together. Combine crab mixture with gelatin, mayonnaise, vinegar, parsley, and relish. Fold in whipped cream. Pour into oiled 6-cup mold and cover with plastic wrap. Chill until firm. Unmold onto large bed of red lettuce leaves. Serve with crackers of choice.

*Yield:* 6 cups

# HASH PINWHEELS WITH SPUNKY CHEESE SAUCE

*Pineapple Inn Bed and Breakfast*

*The Pineapple Inn Bed and Breakfast in Georgetown, Kentucky, offers visitors homemade goods and a full breakfast served in a country French dining room with beautiful table settings. The Inn is furnished with beautiful antiques, and its guests can visit nearby Kentucky Horse Park, Horse Museum, and Keeneland Race Course and take tours of local horse farms.*

*These biscuits are made like a jelly roll filled with hash and are served with cheese sauce.*

### Biscuits

2 cups Bisquick baking mix

½ cup cold water

2 tablespoons solid vegetable shortening

1 (15-ounce) can corned beef or roast beef hash

¼ teaspoon pepper

### Cheese Sauce

2 tablespoons butter or margarine

2 tablespoons Bisquick baking mix

¼ teaspoon salt

¼ teaspoon dry mustard

⅛ teaspoon pepper

1 cup milk

2 ounces cheddar cheese, grated (½ cup)

Preheat oven to 450 degrees. Sift baking mix. Add water and shortening and mix to make soft dough. Gently smooth dough into ball in floured bowl. Cover with a cloth. Knead 5 times. Roll dough into 9 x 12-inch rectangle. Spread hash over dough to within ½ inch of edge. Sprinkle with pepper. Roll up, beginning at narrow side. Cut into nine 1-inch slices. Place slices in greased 9 x 9 x 2-inch pan. Bake for 30 minutes, or until golden brown. Serve hot with cheese sauce on top.

**To make cheese sauce**, melt butter over low heat in saucepan. Blend in baking mix, salt, mustard, and pepper. Cook over low heat, stirring until mixture is smooth and bubbly. Remove from heat and stir in milk. Heat to boiling, stirring constantly. Stir in cheese. Heat until cheese melts.

*Yield:* 6 servings

# SUNDAY MORNING MUFFINS

*Harralson House Inn Bed and Breakfast*

1 cup sour cream

4 tablespoons (½ stick) butter, melted

1 egg, beaten

1 cup bran flakes

1 cup flour

1 teaspoon ground cinnamon

½ teaspoon salt

⅓ cup sugar

¼ teaspoon baking powder

2 small apples, peeled and chopped (about 1 cup)

Preheat oven to 400 degrees. Combine sour cream, butter, and egg. Add bran flakes and let stand until softened. Combine flour, cinnamon, salt, sugar, and baking powder, and add to sour cream mixture, blending just until moistened. Fold in apple pieces. Spoon into lightly greased muffin pan, filling cups three-quarters full. Bake for 25 minutes.

*Yield:* 1 dozen muffins

# ❧ BOSTON BROWN BREAD ❧

3 cups flour

4 teaspoons baking soda

3 teaspoons salt

2 cups wheat germ

2 cups fine graham cracker crumbs

4 eggs, lightly beaten

⅔ cup vegetable oil

2 cups light corn syrup

4 cups buttermilk

Preheat oven to 350 degrees. Sift together flour, baking soda, and salt. Add wheat germ and graham cracker crumbs. In separate bowl mix eggs, oil, corn syrup, and buttermilk and add to flour mixture. Blend with wooden spoon. Grease 4 (1-pound) coffee cans with oil. Fill cans half full of batter and put on baking sheet. Bake for 1 hour, or until a toothpick inserted comes out clean. Cool on wire rack 10 minutes. Run knife around sides of cans and turn out bread. Refrigerate after cooling. Serve with softened cream cheese.

*Yield:* 4 loaves

# FRENCH LENTIL SOUP ✤

*Amelia's Field Country Inn*

*I was referred to Amelia's Field Country Inn in Paris, Kentucky, by Sharon Thompson of the* Lexington Herald-Leader. *The Inn's internationally known chef, Mark May, has won local and national acclaim for his contributions not only to the James Beard Foundation but also to the Inn. Joseph Clay named the Inn for his aunt, Amelia Clay, who inspired him as a child growing up in Kentucky. She would take him to the butcher, show him the difference between good and not-so-good cuts of meat, and teach him the importance of buying only the freshest of ingredients. That tradition lives on at Amelia's Field. Located just thirty minutes from downtown Lexington, this is certainly a trip worth taking.*

1 pound French green dried lentils

1 pound carrots

1 pound onions

1 pound celery stalks

1 clove garlic

6 ounces smoked bacon, cubed

1 tablespoon canola oil

1 sprig fresh rosemary

2 quarts chicken stock or water

1 teaspoon red wine vinegar

Salt and freshly ground pepper

Wash lentils in cold water, checking for pebbles. Drain. Peel carrots and onions, and remove strings from celery. Cut into small dice. Mince garlic. Heat bacon in large saucepan until hot but not smoking. Add vegetables and garlic to bacon, cover, and cook over low heat for about 2 minutes. Do not brown. Add oil and lentils. Continue to cook for 5 minutes. Add rosemary sprig. Add stock slowly. Bring to a boil and simmer slowly for 45 minutes, or until lentils are tender. Remove rosemary sprig and add wine vinegar. Add salt and pepper to taste. Serve hot in soup bowls with nice, warm crusty bread.

*Yield:* 8 to 10 servings

# ∞ COUNTRY HAM ∞ IN CREAM SAUCE ON ENGLISH MUFFINS

4 tablespoons (½ stick) plus 2 teaspoons unsalted butter

4 tablespoons flour

2 cups milk

¼ teaspoon ground nutmeg

Salt and pepper

1 pound cooked country ham, diced

2 teaspoons butter

2 tablespoons snipped fresh chives

5 tablespoons dry sherry

6 toasted English muffin halves

Melt 4 tablespoons butter in saucepan and add flour, stirring well. Add milk and cook over medium heat, stirring constantly, until thickened. Add nutmeg, salt, and pepper to taste. Remove from heat. Simmer country ham in 2 teaspoons butter in skillet for 8 to 10 minutes, stirring occasionally. Add chives. Cook for 3 to 4 more minutes. Add sherry and heat through. Combine ham with cream sauce and serve over toasted English muffin halves.

*Yield:* 6 servings

# COUNTRY HAM SLIVERS
## ON RASPBERRY-LEMON SCONES

2 cups flour

4 teaspoons baking powder

¼ teaspoon baking soda

½ teaspoon salt

2 tablespoons sugar

1½ tablespoons grated lemon peel

5 tablespoons butter, cold

1 cup fresh raspberries

½ cup sour cream

⅓ cup milk

1½ pounds country ham, thinly sliced

Preheat oven to 425 degrees. Combine flour, baking powder, baking soda, salt, sugar, and lemon peel. Cut butter into dry mixture until it resembles coarse crumbs. Fold in raspberries. Combine sour cream and milk and add to raspberry mixture. Turn onto floured surface and roll out to ½-inch thickness. Cut with 2-inch biscuit cutter. Place on ungreased cookie sheet and bake for 15 to 18 minutes, or until golden brown. Split cooled scones and fill with 2 or 3 very thin slices of country ham.

*Yield:* About 2 dozen sandwiches

# PORTABELLA MUSHROOM SANDWICHES

4 unblemished Portabella mushrooms, rinsed and sliced

1 cup Italian dressing

Romaine lettuce leaves

4 slices Muenster or Gruyère cheese

4 fresh bakery rolls (I use snowflake rolls)

Marinate mushroom slices in Italian dressing in refrigerator for at least 2 hours, turning several times. Grill over hot coals until well browned. Place lettuce and cheese on rolls and top with grilled mushrooms.

*Yield:* 4 small sandwiches

# RIBBON SANDWICHES

¼ cup finely chopped fresh basil leaves

¼ cup finely chopped fresh parsley

2 tablespoons plus 1 teaspoon finely snipped fresh chives

4 tablespoons (½ stick) butter, softened

4 ounces cream cheese, softened

Salt and freshly ground pepper

8 thin slices wheat bread, with crusts removed

Combine all ingredients except bread in food processor and blend until smooth and color is green. Spread mixture on 4 slices of bread. Top with remaining slices. Cut each sandwich diagonally into 4 triangles. Assemble on large plate and cover with slightly damp paper towel. Refrigerate until serving time.

*Yield:* 16 small sandwiches

# DELUXE CLUB SANDWICHES

8 slices white bread

½ cup mayonnaise mixed with ½ teaspoon curry powder

8 slices turkey

1 medium cucumber, unpeeled and sliced

8 slices Muenster cheese

Dijon mustard

Leaf lettuce

4 slices wheat bread (I prefer honey wheat)

Trim crusts from bread and spread white slices with curried mayonnaise. Stack half the turkey, cucumber, and Muenster cheese on 4 slices of white bread. Spread cheese with Dijon mustard and top with lettuce and wheat bread. Spread with curried mayonnaise and stack remaining fillings, lettuce, and white bread. Quarter sandwiches and stick a fancy toothpick through each quarter.

*Yield:* 4 servings

# HOT BROWN

*Carrollton Inn*

*The Carrollton Inn is located at Third and Main Streets in Carrollton, Kentucky. It offers us its quick version of the Kentucky hot brown sandwich. It also offers diners very fine dining.*

1 slice toast

4 ounces country ham, thinly sliced

3 ounces turkey breast, thinly sliced

Your favorite cheese sauce

2 slices bacon, cooked and crumbled

1 slice tomato

Preheat broiler. Layer toast, country ham, and turkey breast in ovenproof dish. Top with your favorite cheese sauce. Sprinkle with bacon; top with tomato. Broil for 3 minutes, or until cheese sauce is golden brown and melted.

*Yield:* 1 sandwich

## ❧ MUSHROOMS ON TOAST ❧

Claudia Sanders Dinner House of Shelbyville, Kentucky, Cookbook *by Cherry Settles, Tommy Settles, and Edward G. Klemm*

4 tablespoons water

3 tablespoons butter

¼ teaspoon salt

⅛ teaspoon pepper

1 (6- to 7-ounce) can mushroom caps, drained

2 slices white toast brushed with melted butter

Heat water in skillet. Add and melt butter. Season with salt and pepper and mix thoroughly. Add mushroom caps. Fry over moderate heat for about 5 minutes, stirring often. Place caps on buttered toast and pour any remaining liquid from skillet over them.

*Yield:* 2 generous servings

# ❧ THE BOUNTY ❧

*Lynn's Paradise Café*

*This is absolutely the most wonderful sandwich, and the wheat berry bread makes it super special.*

**Bounty Mix**

1 pound softened cream cheese

½ medium red onion, diced small

1 large cucumber, peeled, seeded, and diced small

Pinch of salt

Pinch of white pepper

Mix all ingredients thoroughly.

*Yield:* enough to make 6 to 8 sandwiches

**For each sandwich you will need**

2 slices wheat berry bread, toasted

2 to 3 slices roasted turkey breast

3 to 4 slices tomato

1 or 2 large leaves leaf lettuce

Mayonnaise

Dijon mustard

Layer sandwich on toasted bread in the following order: On bottom slice spread ⅓ cup of the Bounty mix, then top with turkey breast, sliced tomato, and lettuce. Generously spread top slice of toast with mayonnaise and mustard. Close sandwich and cut in half diagonally.

# CANADIAN BACON SOUFFLÉ

½ cup solid vegetable shortening

½ cup flour

2 cups milk

6 egg yolks, well beaten

5 ounces mild cheddar cheese, grated (1¼ cups)

½ teaspoon salt

½ teaspoon freshly ground pepper

¼ teaspoon Tabasco

⅔ cup lightly cooked and cubed Canadian bacon

7 egg whites

4 paper-thin slices Swiss or Gruyère cheese

Preheat oven to 375 degrees. Grease 2-quart casserole. In saucepan blend shortening and flour until crumbly. Stir in milk and bring to a boil. Reduce heat and stir until mixture is very thick and pulling away from sides of pan. Remove from heat and let stand 2 minutes. Add egg yolks. Stir in cheddar cheese, salt, pepper, Tabasco, and bacon. Beat egg whites until they form stiff peaks. Fold in gently. Spoon mixture into casserole. Cover with Swiss cheese. Bake for 25 to 30 minutes.

*Yield:* 4 servings

# EGG SALAD WITH BACON AND COUNTRY HAM

Claudia Sanders Dinner House of Shelbyville, Kentucky,
Cookbook *by Cherry Settles, Tommy Settles, and Edward G. Klemm*

6 hard-boiled eggs, grated or finely chopped
¼ cup crisply cooked and crumbled bacon
¼ cup ground Claudia Sanders Kentucky Country Ham
1 teaspoon minced onion
½ cup finely chopped celery
½ teaspoon seasoned salt
¼ teaspoon Tabasco
¼ cup mayonnaise
1 tablespoon lemon juice or cider vinegar
Paprika for garnish
6 stuffed olives (chopped or whole, to top each serving)

Mix all ingredients except lemon juice and olives thoroughly. Garnish with lemon juice and olives.

*Yield:* About 6 servings (6 sandwiches)

# CHEESE-STUFFED TOAST

*Jailer's Inn Bed and Breakfast*

*The Jailer's Inn Bed and Breakfast in Bardstown, Kentucky,
is absolutely one of the most fun places to visit and tour when you
need a dose of Kentucky history. You can sleep over in
an actual jail cell there, and the owners truly pamper their guests
with great dishes like this one.*

10 slices French bread, 2 inches thick
3 tablespoons plus 1 teaspoon strawberry preserves

6 ounces cream cheese, cubed into 10 pieces

5 eggs

1 cup milk

¼ pound (1 stick) butter, melted

¼ cup maple syrup

Dash of ground nutmeg

Preheat oven to 350 degrees. Cut out a pocket about the size of a silver dollar in each piece of bread. Fill pockets with 1 tablespoon preserves and 1 cube cream cheese. Replace bread pieces in pockets and press together lightly. Place in greased 13 x 9 x 2-inch baking dish. Blend eggs, milk, butter, maple syrup, and nutmeg. Pour over bread slices and refrigerate overnight. Bake for 40 minutes, or until golden brown. Serve with maple syrup or melted preserves.

*Yield:* 8 to 10 servings

## ✠ PIMIENTO AND ✠ GREEN CHILI QUICHE

6 large eggs

1¼ cups sour cream

1 tablespoon cream or dry sherry

½ cup pimientos, drained and chopped

¾ cup green chilies, drained and chopped

2 tablespoons dried onion

6 ounces cheddar cheese, grated (1½ cups)

1 (9-inch) pie shell, unbaked

Preheat oven to 425 degrees. Mix together eggs, sour cream, and sherry. Add pimientos, chilies, and onion. Mix well. Add cheese. Pour into pie shell and bake for 40 to 45 minutes, or until golden brown. Serve warm.

*Yield:* 8 servings

# ANISE TEA COOKIES

1 cup solid vegetable shortening

1 cup light brown sugar (packed)

1 cup honey

1 cup sour cream

3 eggs

3½ cups flour

2 teaspoons baking soda

1 teaspoon aniseed

¼ teaspoon salt

Preheat oven to 350 degrees. Cream shortening and brown sugar until well blended. Add honey, sour cream, and eggs, beating well. Combine flour, baking soda, aniseed, and salt. Add to creamed mixture, blending well. Drop by teaspoonfuls onto greased cookie sheet. Bake for 10 to 13 minutes, until lightly browned. Cool on wire rack.

*Yield:* 7 to 8 dozen cookies

# RUSSIAN TEA CAKES

½ pound (2 sticks) unsalted butter

½ cup powdered sugar

1½ teaspoons vanilla extract

2¼ cups flour

¼ teaspoon salt

⅓ cup chopped pecans

Powdered sugar

Preheat oven to 400 degrees. Cream butter, powdered sugar, and vanilla extract. Stir flour and salt together and add to butter mixture.

Stir in pecans and chill thoroughly. Form chilled dough into 1-inch balls and bake on ungreased cookie sheet for 10 to 12 minutes. Cakes will be set but not brown. Cool slightly and roll warm cookies in powdered sugar. Cool and roll in sugar again.

*Yield:* 4 dozen tea cakes

## ❧ STRAWBERRIES ❧ TOPPED WITH CUSTARD

½ cup sugar

2½ tablespoons cornstarch

1½ cups milk

4 eggs, beaten

½ cup sour cream

1½ teaspoons vanilla extract

ice water

1½ pints fresh strawberries, washed, hulled, and halved

Combine sugar and cornstarch in medium saucepan. Gradually stir in milk and cook over medium heat, stirring constantly, until it boils. Boil and stir 1 minute. Remove from heat. Add beaten eggs to milk mixture in saucepan and blend. Add sour cream and vanilla extract and beat with whisk until well blended. Cool immediately by placing in bowl of ice water for several minutes. Cover and chill thoroughly. To serve, spoon custard sauce over strawberries.

*Yield:* 4 servings

# PANACHUKEN WITH ORANGE SYRUP

*Shepherd Place Bed and Breakfast*

*While visiting Shepherd Place Bed and Breakfast, a pre<n>Civil War home in Versailles, Kentucky, built around 1815, take the opportunity to relax and pet the resident ewes, Abigail and Victoria. You may also want to commission owner Sylvia Yawn to knit you a sweater out of yarn you select. Whatever you decide to do while you visit Shepherd Place in the heart of bluegrass country, just ten minutes from downtown Lexington and four miles from Keeneland, you'll be glad you came to visit.*

### Panachuken
2 tablespoons butter

½ cup milk

2 eggs

½ cup flour

Dash of salt

### Orange Syrup
1 (12-ounce) can frozen orange juice

1½ cups sugar

1½ cups light corn syrup

½ teaspoon ground nutmeg

Preheat oven to 450 degrees. Melt butter in pie plate in oven. Beat together milk, eggs, flour, and salt. Pour into pie plate and bake until brown and fluffy. Serve with orange syrup.

**To make orange syrup,** put all ingredients in 2-quart saucepan. Heat and stir until orange juice and sugar are melted. Serve warm.

*Yield:* 6 to 8 servings

*Note:* If desired, before baking the panachuken, top it with nuts or fruit. This recipe for orange syrup makes a lot, and it will save well in the refrigerator.

# BAKED LUNCHEON FRUIT

1 (15-ounce) can apricot halves, drained

1 (1-pound) can purple plums, drained

1 (1-pound) can peach halves, drained

4 thin slices navel orange, halved

¼ cup light brown sugar

½ cup orange juice

½ teaspoon finely grated lemon zest

2 tablespoons butter, melted

½ cup flaked coconut

Preheat oven to 400 degrees. Arrange apricots and plums in shallow baking dish. Alternate peach halves with orange slices for next layer. Mix brown sugar, juice, and lemon zest and pour over fruit. Drizzle butter and sprinkle coconut over entire dish. Bake for 20 minutes.

*Yield:* 8 to 10 servings

# SWEET POTATO SALAD

5 to 6 sweet potatoes, baked

1 (15-ounce) can pineapple chunks, drained

1½ cups halved strawberries

½ cup blueberries

1 cup chopped pecans

1 cup flaked coconut

2 cups miniature marshmallows

1 (8-ounce) tub whipped topping

Lettuce leaves

Cool, peel, and dice sweet potatoes. Add pineapple, strawberries, blueberries, pecans, coconut, and marshmallows and fold in whipped topping. Mix well and chill. Serve on lettuce leaves.

*Yield:* 8 servings

# Soups and Salads

# Soups and Salads

 Alma Louise Harbin, a celebrated Kentucky cook, has cooked for more than fifty years. She wins county and state fair ribbons with an unbelievable ease. She tells of a time when she was fifteen and anxious to impress her boyfriend, Ellsworth. She invited him for dinner and prepared potato salad, hoping that the way to a man's heart was really through his stomach. What Alma didn't know as she sat down to the dinner she had prepared was that the small onions she took from the cellar were actually gladiola bulbs. Eight brothers and sisters teased her about her efforts, and Ellsworth survived. They have been married for more than fifty years, and Alma remains a true cooking legend in Bullitt County, Kentucky.

Nothing warms the heart and the kitchen as much as a bowl of hot soup. I admit that I am a soup connoisseur and love to begin cooking on a cold rainy day with a rich stock, some wine, and no idea what delicious concoction will result in the pot that evening. I have offered you my favorites from a collection of soup recipes created over the years and recipes sent to me by readers. A soup can be the ultimate comfort food. I have learned over the years that the aroma of a good soup simmering will surely bring the family running to the table.

Salads should be exciting. We've become so accustomed to the lettuce-and-tomato variety that we often overlook other possibilities. One of my favorite salad varieties is the Dandelion Salad included here, which my grandmother used to prepare when I was very young. I would watch as she picked dandelions at just the right stage--when they were young and tender, before they fully bloomed. When too old, the dandelion becomes quite bitter. She would wash them thoroughly, cut them into pieces, and add hard-boiled eggs and crumbled bacon. I've added my own raspberry vinaigrette and homemade garlic-seasoned croutons for a readily available spring dish well worth trying.

Rarely do I use iceberg lettuce. As a caterer I discovered the beauty of deep purple and red lettuce varieties to display on my buffet tables under silver trays filled with elegant dishes. I also use them under tropical fruits and fruit kabobs served with Devonshire dip. I find the purple savoy and tart radicchio types both appealing to the eye and very tasty. Experiment with different lettuces, and use glass bowls whenever possible. When adding garlic to my salads, I like to rub the inside of the bowl or individual plates with a clove to give flavor but not overpower.

Fresh fruits and vegetable salads are only as limited as your imagination. Many salad recipes I've collected throughout the years indicate that Kentucky cooks have great imagination when it comes to exciting salads. I often use ingredients such as jicama, hearts of palm, star fruit, and strips of mesquite-marinated steak in my own recipes. A salad can be nearly a meal in itself, such as the Cobb Salad served with a loaf of crusty bread. And light, summertime lunches can consist mainly of a recipe of pasta, congealed fruit or melon, and tuna. Take advantage of fruits and vegetables in season, and always use them at the height of their freshness. Salads are not only beautiful but can be a light, tasty addition to any meal.

# CREAM OF ASPARAGUS SOUP

2 tablespoons unsalted butter
1 small onion, chopped
1 stalk celery, chopped
2 cups beef stock
1 pound tender young asparagus
1 cup light whipping cream
Salt
Freshly ground pepper

Heat butter in medium saucepan and cook onion and celery until softened. Stir frequently; do not brown. Add stock and bring to a boil. Add trimmed asparagus to liquid and cook over low heat for 5 minutes. Pour into blender and process until liquid. Add cream. Salt and pepper to taste and serve.

*Yield:* 6 servings

# ELEGANT CRAB SOUP

3 tablespoons unsalted butter
1 tablespoon flour
3 cups half-and-half
1 teaspoon salt
Freshly ground pepper
½ tablespoon Worcestershire sauce
2 tablespoons grated onion
3 tablespoons dry sherry
1 pound crabmeat, shredded

Melt butter in soup pan. Over medium heat add flour and stir well to blend. Slowly add half-and-half, salt, pepper, Worcestershire sauce, onion, and sherry. Do not boil. Add crab and reduce heat. Simmer 30 minutes, stirring frequently.

*Yield:* 4 servings

# ☙ MY FAVORITE ☙
# OYSTERCHOKE SOUP

*During my years as a restaurant critic in Texas I often visited a favorite cajun restaurant. They served the best artichoke-oyster soup to be found anywhere. After many tries I have duplicated as closely as possible that wonderful flavor.*

¼ pound (1 stick) unsalted butter

1½ cups chopped green onions with tops

2 cloves garlic, crushed

3 tablespoons flour

3 (14-ounce) cans artichoke hearts, drained and chopped

6 cups chicken stock

½ teaspoon crushed red pepper

1 teaspoon salt

1 quart fresh oysters, chopped, with liquid reserved

Melt butter in heavy Dutch oven. Add onions and garlic and sauté for 4 minutes. Add flour and cook for 5 minutes, stirring constantly. Stir in artichokes, chicken stock, red pepper, and salt and cook over low heat for 20 minutes. Add oysters and their liquid and simmer 10 more minutes. Do not overcook.

*Yield:* 10 servings

# SUPER CHEESE SOUP

4 tablespoons (½ stick) butter or margarine
¼ cup plus 2 tablespoons flour
2 (10¾-ounce) cans chicken broth, undiluted
2 cups milk
¼ teaspoon white pepper
2 tablespoons chopped pimiento
¼ cup plus 2 tablespoons dry white wine
½ teaspoon Worcestershire sauce
¼ teaspoon hot sauce
½ pound sharp cheddar cheese, grated (2 cups)

Melt butter in heavy saucepan over low heat and add flour, stirring until smooth. Cook for 1 minute, stirring constantly. Gradually add broth and milk and cook over medium heat, stirring constantly, until thickened and bubbly. Stir in white pepper. Add pimiento, wine, Worcestershire sauce, and hot sauce. Heat to boiling, stirring frequently. Remove from heat. Add cheese and stir until cheese melts. Serve immediately.

*Yield:* 5 cups

# MINESTRONE

⅓ cup olive oil

3 tablespoons butter

2 medium onions, chopped fine

3 carrots, chopped

1 medium potato, cubed

3 stalks celery, chopped

¼ pound green beans, cut into 1-inch pieces

2 medium zucchini, peeled and cubed

½ pound cabbage, shredded

2 small cloves garlic, minced

1 can (about 28 ounces) Italian-style tomatoes with liquid

3½ cups beef stock

2 cups water

½ teaspoon dried crushed basil

¼ teaspoon dried crushed rosemary

1 bay leaf

Salt and pepper

Freshly grated Parmesan cheese

Heat oil and butter in 6-quart Dutch oven over medium heat. Add onions and sauté, stirring frequently, 6 to 8 minutes, until soft and golden. Stir in carrots and potato. Continue cooking 5 minutes longer, stirring constantly. Add celery and green beans, cooking and stirring an additional 5 minutes. Add zucchini, cabbage, and garlic, cooking and stirring 5 more minutes.

Drain tomatoes, reserving liquid. Add stock, water, and reserved liquid to Dutch oven. Chop tomatoes coarsely and add to pot. Stir in basil, rosemary, and bay leaf. Salt and pepper to taste. Bring to boil over high heat and reduce to low. Cover and simmer about 1½ hours, stirring occasionally. Remove bay leaf. Ladle into bowls and sprinkle with cheese.

*Yield:* 8 to 10 servings

# FRENCH ONION SOUP

8 large onions, thinly sliced

¾ cup olive oil

3 quarts beef stock

1 bay leaf

1½ teaspoons salt

1 teaspoon freshly ground pepper

½ cup red wine

6 slices toasted French bread

4 ounces Gruyère or Swiss cheese, freshly grated (1 cup)

Cook onions in oil until golden brown. Pour off oil. Add beef stock, bay leaf, salt, and pepper. Cook over low heat for 1½ hours. Remove from heat and add wine. Remove bay leaf. Pour soup into 6 ovenproof serving dishes. Place 1 slice of French bread in each bowl and sprinkle cheese on top of bread. Put bowls under broiler until cheese melts.

*Yield:* 6 servings

# ITALIAN MEATBALL SOUP

2½ pounds beef bones

3 stalks celery

3 carrots

1 medium onion, halved

1 bay leaf

6 cups cold water

1 egg

4 tablespoons chopped fresh parsley

1 teaspoon salt

½ teaspoon crushed marjoram

½ teaspoon pepper

½ cup fresh bread crumbs

⅓ cup Parmesan cheese

1 pound ground chuck

1 (14½-ounce) can whole peeled tomatoes with liquid

⅔ cup penne pasta or rotini pasta

Rinse bones and combine with celery, carrots, onion, and bay leaf in 6-quart Dutch oven. Add 6 cups cold water and bring to a boil. Reduce heat to low. Cover and simmer about 1 hour, skimming foam frequently. Preheat oven to 400 degrees. Spray 13 x 9 x 2-inch baking pan with nonstick spray. Combine egg, 3 tablespoons of the parsley, ½ teaspoon of the salt, marjoram, and ¼ teaspoon of the pepper in medium bowl. Add bread crumbs and cheese. Add beef and mix well. Put mixture on cutting board and pat evenly into large square 1 inch thick. With sharp knife cut meat into 1-inch-square pieces. Shape into balls. Place in prepared pan and bake for 20 to 25 minutes, until brown and thoroughly cooked, turning occasionally. Drain on paper towels.

Strain prepared stock and let sit for 10 minutes. Remove grease by pulling clean paper towels across surface.

Slice celery and carrots and discard bones, onion, and bay leaf. Return stock to pot. Drain tomatoes, reserving liquid. Chop tomatoes and add to stock with liquid. Bring to a boil, uncover, and boil for 5 minutes. Stir in pasta, remaining ½ teaspoon salt, and remaining ¼ teaspoon pepper and continue cooking for 5 minutes, stirring frequently. Add celery, carrots, and meatballs and reduce to medium heat. Cook 10 minutes longer. Stir in remaining 1 tablespoon parsley and add more salt and pepper to taste if necessary.

*Yield:* 6 servings

## ❧ MUSHROOM SOUP ❧

*This is a favorite of mine. When my friend Sue Ann Harmon and I are down or having a bad day, a pot of this soup and a loaf of fresh bread help us soar to new heights.*

4 medium onions, minced

2 cloves garlic, minced

4 tablespoons (½ stick) butter or margarine

2 pounds fresh mushrooms, chopped

2 cups light whipping cream

2 cups beef stock

1 cup Parmesan cheese

1 cup sliced almonds, toasted

Chopped fresh parsley

Sauté onions and garlic in butter in Dutch oven over medium heat until onions are tender. Add mushrooms and cook over low heat for 10 minutes, or until tender. Gradually add cream and stock. Continue cooking until thoroughly heated. Do not boil. Sprinkle each serving with cheese, almonds, and parsley.

*Yield:* 2½ quarts

# HOMEMADE BEEF ✿ VEGETABLE SOUP

*Alma Warren*

*Many people love chicken soup when they're feeling under the weather. Not me. When I feel a cold coming on or when I just need a good pick-me-up, I want homemade vegetable soup, and nobody makes it better than my mother's friend Alma Warren. It's also great with a couple of cups of cooked macaroni added, but, as Alma says, "make sure you have a soup bone as it is what makes the soup so delicious."*

1 quart water

3 pounds beef with bone in or soup bones

1 (46-ounce) can tomato juice

2 (15-ounce) cans tomatoes, drained

1 (15-ounce) can green beans, drained

1 (15-ounce) can corn, drained

1 (15-ounce) can peas, drained

4 cups chopped onions

4 cups diced potatoes

1 cup diced turnips

1 cup diced celery

1 cup chopped okra

Salt to taste

In dutch oven, cook beef in water until tender and remove from stock. Add all other ingredients to beef stock and cook until almost tender. Add cut-up beef and continue cooking until vegetables are tender.

*Yield:* 10 servings

# AMBROSIA

4 seedless oranges, peeled, sectioned, and sections halved

2 cups pineapple chunks

1 banana, peeled and sliced

2 teaspoons lemon juice

½ cup flaked coconut

½ cup light whipping cream

4 teaspoons powdered sugar

¾ cup mayonnaise

Combine orange, pineapple, and banana pieces in large bowl. Drizzle with lemon juice and lightly toss. Sprinkle coconut over mixture. Before serving, whip cream with powdered sugar until stiff. Fold in mayonnaise, and fold mixture into fruit mix. Serve immediately.

*Yield:* 6 servings

# WINED FRUIT MOLD

1 (6-ounce) package and 1 (3-ounce) package raspberry gelatin

3 cups boiling water

1 cup port wine

1 large can crushed pineapple, drained

¾ cup chopped pecans

1 cup chopped celery

Dissolve gelatin in 3 cups boiling water. Cool until slightly thickened. Stir in wine, pineapple, pecans, and celery. Pour into large mold or 13 x 9 x 2-inch glass dish greased with mayonnaise. Chill until firm. Serve on lettuce leaves.

*Yield:* 6 servings

# WALDORF SALAD

4 large tart red apples, unpeeled and diced

2 stalks celery, diced

½ cup miniature marshmallows

1 cup seedless grapes

½ cup chopped pecans

1 (3-ounce) package cream cheese, softened

1 tablespoon sugar

¾ cup mayonnaise

½ cup whipped topping

Combine apples, celery, marshmallows, grapes, and pecans in large bowl. Beat cream cheese, sugar, and mayonnaise until creamy. Fold in whipped topping and fold into fruit mixture. Cover and refrigerate until serving time. Place on individual plates atop lettuce leaves.

*Yield:* 4 to 6 servings

# WILTED LETTUCE SALAD

4 cups torn romaine lettuce

4 small green onions with tops, chopped

4 slices bacon

4 tablespoons cider vinegar

4 teaspoons light brown sugar

Salt and pepper

Put lettuce and onion in large bowl. Chop bacon and brown until crisp. Add vinegar and brown sugar to hot bacon and grease. Salt and pepper to taste. Pour immediately over lettuce and onions. Toss and serve.

*Yield:* 4 to 6 servings

# DANDELION SALAD

### Salad

1 pound dandelion stems
2 hard-boiled eggs, chopped
4 slices bacon, cooked and crumbled
Garlic-seasoned croutons (see note)

### Vinaigrette

6 tablespoons olive oil
2 tablespoons raspberry vinegar
Pinch of sugar
Salt and freshly ground pepper to taste

Mix dandelion pieces with eggs and bacon. Top with croutons and vinaigrette.

**To make vinaigrette,** beat all ingredients together.

*Yield:* 4 servings

*Note:* I use French bread cut into cubes, lightly tossed with butter and minced garlic, and toasted to make my seasoned croutons.

# RADICCHIO CHIFFONADE

1 tablespoon white wine vinegar

1 tablespoon fresh lemon juice

1 hard-boiled egg, finely chopped

¼ cup olive oil

1 tablespoon snipped fresh chives

1 teaspoon chopped fresh parsley

Pinch of sugar

⅛ teaspoon salt

Freshly ground pepper

3 small heads radicchio, torn into small pieces

In small jar, combine vinegar, lemon juice, half the egg, oil, chives, parsley, sugar, salt, and pepper. Cover and shake well. Just before serving pour over radicchio and toss until coated. Sprinkle with remaining half of egg.

*Yield:* 4 servings


# RED LETTUCE
# WITH CREAMY DIJON DRESSING

1 tablespoon sour cream

2 tablespoons Dijon mustard

1 tablespoon red wine vinegar

½ teaspoon salt

½ cup salad oil

1 head red leaf lettuce, washed and torn into small pieces

3 tablespoons chopped green onions with tops

½ cucumber, cut into small chunks

Combine sour cream, mustard, vinegar, and salt and mix well. Slowly beat in oil until thickened. Pour into container with tight-fitting lid and store in refrigerator until ready to use. Assemble lettuce, onions, and cucumber in glass bowl and toss with dressing just before serving.

*Yield:* 2 servings

## ❧ BEET SALAD ❧ WITH RED ONIONS

1 (15-ounce) can sliced beets, drained

¼ large red onion

2 tablespoons red wine vinegar

3 tablespoons corn oil

Freshly ground pepper

Put beets in salad bowl. Slice onion lengthwise into very thin strips and add to beets. Add vinegar, oil, and pepper. Toss. Let sit for 30 minutes before serving.

*Yield:* 4 servings

# CUCUMBER LIME SALAD

*Harralson House Inn Bed and Breakfast*

1½ cups boiling water

1 (6-ounce) package lime gelatin

1 cup Miracle Whip salad dressing

1 cup diced cucumber

2 tablespoons minced onion

2 tablespoons distilled white vinegar

1 tablespoon horseradish

Add boiling water to gelatin and mix well. Chill until gelatin begins to thicken. Add salad dressing and whip until blended. Add other ingredients and chill until firm.

*Yield:* 6 servings

# MY FAVORITE BROCCOLI SALAD

*My friend Millie Philips of Arlington, Texas, served this
at a dinner party I attended. It added a whole new dimension
to my love for good salads.*

1 medium head fresh broccoli and stems, trimmed and chopped

½ cup sunflower seeds

½ cup raisins

6 slices bacon, cooked and crumbled

¾ cup Miracle Whip salad dressing

⅓ cup sugar

2 tablespoons cider vinegar

Combine broccoli, sunflower seeds, raisins, and bacon. Combine salad dressing with sugar and vinegar. Toss with broccoli mixture.

*Yield:* 6 servings

## ✹ SUMMER SALAD ✹

2 cups chopped ripe tomatoes

1 cup thickly sliced, peeled cucumber

1 (3-ounce) can sliced mushrooms with liquid

1 scant teaspoon salt

Freshly ground pepper

3 tablespoons vegetable oil

1 clove garlic, minced

3 tablespoons red wine vinegar

Lettuce

3 tablespoons crumbled bleu cheese

Put tomatoes, cucumber, and mushrooms, including liquid, in bowl. Combine salt, pepper, oil, garlic, and wine vinegar and pour over vegetables. Chill for several hours. To serve, place mixture on lettuce leaves and sprinkle with cheese.

*Yield:* 4 servings

# COBB SALAD

1 small head iceberg lettuce

½ head romaine lettuce

½ bunch of watercress

3 small tomatoes, peeled

2 whole chicken breasts, roasted

6 slices bacon, cooked crisp

1 avocado, peeled

3 hard-boiled eggs, chopped

1 teaspoon snipped fresh chives

2 ounces Roquefort cheese, grated (½ cup)

1 cup French dressing

Chop iceberg lettuce, romaine lettuce, and watercress very fine. Toss and arrange in large bowl. Cut tomatoes in quarters, dice, and arrange in strip across salad. Dice chicken breasts and arrange over top of chopped salad greens. Crumble bacon and sprinkle over salad. Cut avocado in long, thin strips and arrange around outer edge of salad. Sprinkle chopped eggs, chives, and cheese over salad. Pour dressing over all.

*Yield:* 4 to 6 servings

# GERMAN POTATO SALAD

½ pound sliced bacon, cut into ½-inch pieces

¼ cup flour

¾ cup cider vinegar

1 cup water

1 cup sugar

1 large, mild onion, finely chopped

4 to 6 large potatoes

Salt and pepper

¼ teaspoon celery seed

Fry bacon until crisp and remove from fat. Stir flour, vinegar, water, and sugar into fat and simmer for 10 minutes. Add onion and simmer 5 minutes longer. Boil potatoes whole in skins until tender. Peel and thinly slice. Put potatoes in serving bowl and add salt, pepper, and celery seed. Sprinkle bacon pieces over potatoes and pour liquid mixture over all. Serve warm or at room temperature.

*Yield:* 4 to 6 servings

## ◈ TOMATO, MOZZARELLA, ◈ AND BASIL SALAD

3 tablespoons red wine vinegar

2 small cloves garlic, minced

½ teaspoon salt

Freshly ground pepper

½ teaspoon dry mustard

⅓ cup olive oil

5 Italian plum tomatoes

6 ounces mozzarella cheese

10 fresh basil leaves

Combine vinegar, garlic, salt, pepper, and mustard in small bowl. Add oil in steady stream, whisking until thoroughly blended. Cut tomatoes and mozzarella cheese into ¼-inch-thick slices. Place tomato and cheese slices in large bowl and pour dressing over them. Cover and marinate in refrigerator for at least 1 hour. Turn often. With scissors, cut basil leaves into long, narrow strips. Alternate tomato and cheese slices on large serving plate and sprinkle with basil. Drizzle with dressing from marinade.

*Yield:* 4 servings

# CHICKEN SALAD
# WITH COUNTRY DRESSING

*Shaker Village of Pleasant Hill*

*From* We Make You Kindly Welcome *by Elizabeth C. Kremer*

**Chicken Salad**

1 pound cooked chicken

¾ cup chopped celery

¼ teaspoon seasoned salt

¼ teaspoon salt

¼ teaspoon crushed red pepper

¼ cup mayonnaise

¼ cup chopped pecans

**Country Dressing**

1 teaspoon dry mustard

2 tablespoons sugar

¼ teaspoon salt

2 tablespoons flour

½ cup cold water

2 egg yolks

¼ cup distilled white vinegar

2 tablespoons butter

**To make Country Dressing,** dissolve mustard, sugar, salt, and flour in ½ cup cold water. Beat egg yolks and vinegar in top of double boiler. Add dissolved ingredients. Cook and stir dressing over boiling water until thick and smooth. Add butter.

**To make salad,** cut chicken into cubes with scissors and mix with celery and seasoned salt, salt, and crushed red pepper. Fold in ¾ cup Country Dressing, then mayonnaise and pecans. Top with mayonnaise when serving.

*Yield:* 4 to 6 servings

# Desserts

# Desserts

 It's a wonder Ellissa Geary ever became a good Kentucky cook. When she was twelve she begged her mother, Linda Neal, "Let me make dessert for supper." She was intent on doing it all by herself and shooed everyone out of the kitchen when it came time to prepare her peach pie.

After the meal everyone ooohed and aaahed at the dessert she had made. Her mother attests that it was picture perfect and looked as though it would be delicious. Everyone was poised with fork in hand, and all took their first bite at the same time. Ellissa burst into tears as everyone also spit out their bites of peach pie at the same time and yelled, "Yukkk!"

The young cook had used salt instead of sugar for the peach pie filling.

I could write all day on the history of desserts in my family. I grew up believing that it was no special trick for any mom to whip up cream puffs, butter danish, and French crullers, as my own mother did it on a regular basis. We never knew what would be waiting as an after-school treat, but we always knew it would be homemade and it would be delicious.

My uncle Vincent has served in many renowned places as executive pastry chef, and he is responsible for many good recipes in this cookbook. When I visit him in Florida I always anticipate the most scrumptious cheesecakes, napoleons, and charlottes to be found anywhere. I have spent years collecting and improving on the dessert recipes found in this chapter.

Whether they be simple or spectacular, I want my desserts to make a statement. I want dessert to leave my guests with a sense of the extraordinary even when it is a simple lemon pie. That sense is what I find in Kentucky desserts, both the lavish and the more simple traditional dishes. My grandmother's Egg Custard Pie is considered a simple dessert, but it has the texture of velvet. The White Chocolate Cake with Cream Cheese Icing is more time consuming but truly worth the effort.

While today's busy lifestyles don't always allow us to prepare dessert, and fat grams are certainly a valid reason for not eating dessert too often, I hope you enjoy some of what I consider to be just a sampling of great endings to great Kentucky meals.

# CHESS PIE

*The Old Talbott Tavern*

*Old Talbott Tavern has long been one of my favorite Kentucky restaurants. When I was a child my grandmother would take me to Bardstown to get a slice of what she called "the best pie to be found." I still enjoy meals at the Tavern whenever I visit Bardstown. If you're fortunate enough to dine there, do try the pies! My grandmother was right.*

¼ pound (1 stick) margarine

2½ cups sugar

⅛ cup self-rising flour

½ pinch of salt

4 eggs

½ tablespoon vanilla extract

1 cup whole milk

2 (9-inch) pie shells, unbaked

Preheat oven to 375 degrees.

Cream together margarine and sugar, gradually adding self-rising flour, salt, and eggs. Add vanilla extract and milk and beat only until ingredients are mixed. Pour into pie shells and bake for 10 minutes or until center is set. Reduce temperature to 350 degrees and continue baking for 25 minutes.

*Yield:* Two 9-inch pies

# BLUEBERRY CREAM PIE

*Alma Harbin*

*Alma Harbin is a well-known cook in Bullitt County. The day I visited her home to interview her for* Kentucky Living, *she had just entered this pie in the state fair. She made one for us, and I enjoyed two pieces before leaving the kitchen table. She makes piecrust making seem like an art.*

### Double-Crust Pie Shell
2 cups all-purpose flour

1 teaspoon salt

⅔ cup solid vegetable shortening

3 to 6 tablespoons cold water

### Filling
¾ cup sugar

4 tablespoons all-purpose flour

½ teaspoon salt

¾ cup light whipping cream

3 cups blueberries

**To make 9-inch pie shell,** sift flour and salt together and add shortening. Cut in with pastry blender or fork until pieces are the size of small peas. Add cold water by teaspoonfuls, tossing with fork until all the flour-coated bits of shortening are barely dampened.

Turn mixture onto square of waxed paper. Gather up the corners, pressing from the outside to form a compact ball. Divide for lower and upper crusts. Chill for easier handling.

Roll pastry ⅛ inch thick, rolling from center to outer edges. Trim crust around edges, leaving about ¾ inch to fold under for fluting. Repeat with remaining dough for top crust.

**To make pie,** Preheat oven to 425 degrees. Line 9-inch pie plate with 1 pie shell. Trim and turn edges; flute edges. Put berries in pie shell. Combine sugar, flour, and salt in mixing bowl. Mix with cream. Pour mixture over berries. Cut second pie shell into your favorite design or shapes. Arrange on top of pie and crimp edges to seal. Bake for 10 minutes; then reduce temperature to 325 degrees and bake for 35 more minutes.

*Yield:* 8 servings

## ✆ BUTTERMILK PIE ✆

2 eggs, beaten

1 cup sugar

2 tablespoons butter, softened

½ teaspoon salt

1 teaspoon vanilla extract

2 tablespoons all-purpose flour

1 cup buttermilk

Dash of ground nutmeg

1 (9-inch) pie shell, unbaked

Preheat oven to 400 degrees.

Beat eggs and sugar together. Add butter, salt, vanilla extract, flour, and buttermilk and pour into pie shell. Sprinkle with nutmeg. Bake for 10 minutes. Reduce heat to 350 degrees and bake for 30 more minutes, or until firm.

*Yield:* 8 servings

# ❧ THE RICHEST ❧ BUTTERSCOTCH PIE

### Filling

1 cup light brown sugar (packed)

½ cup all-purpose flour

¼ teaspoon salt

1 (13-ounce) can evaporated milk

4 egg yolks (set aside whites for meringue)

4 tablespoons (½ stick) unsalted butter

1 teaspoon vanilla extract

Prebaked 9-inch pie shell

### Meringue

4 egg whites

⅛ teaspoon salt

½ cup sugar

¼ teaspoon cream of tartar

Put brown sugar, flour, and salt in bowl. Add enough water to evaporated milk to make 2 cups. In separate bowl lightly beat egg yolks and whisk in ½ cup of milk mixture. Stir egg mixture into dry ingredients until thoroughly blended. Add rest of milk mixture.

Pour into double boiler and cook over medium heat, stirring constantly, until very thick. Remove from heat and stir in butter and vanilla extract. Cover with waxed paper and cool for 12 to 15 minutes. Pour filling into pie shell and cover again with waxed paper. Chill for 3 hours.

Preheat oven to 350 degrees.

**To make meringue,** beat egg whites in small bowl until foamy. Gradually beat in salt, sugar, and cream of tartar and continue beating until stiff peaks form. Spread meringue over pie, making sure edges are sealed. Bake for 10 to 12 minutes, until peaks of meringue are golden brown. Chill for several hours before serving.

*Yield:* 8 servings

# ❧ CUSTARD PIE ❧

*Cissy Gregg,* Louisville Courier-Journal

1 (9-inch) pie shell, unbaked

4 eggs (or 2 eggs and 4 egg yolks), slightly beaten

½ cup sugar

⅛ teaspoon salt

¼ teaspoon vanilla extract

½ teaspoon almond extract

2½ cups milk, scalded

Ground nutmeg

Line pie plate with pie shell. Be sure there are no bubbles under pastry and no holes in it. For best results, make pastry thicker than usual. Place in refrigerator while preparing filling.

Preheat oven to 325 degrees.

Blend eggs, sugar, salt, and extracts. Slowly pour milk into egg mixture, stirring constantly. Pour into pie shell. Bake for 30 to 40 minutes, or until knife inserted halfway between outside and center of custard comes out clean. Remove promptly to cooling rack. Do not cut pie until just before serving. Sprinkle with nutmeg, if desired.

*Yield:* 8 servings

# COCONUT CREAM PIE

*Elk Creek Restaurant, Yvonne Patterson, owner*

*The Elk Creek Restaurant opened twenty-four years ago as just a grill area. It's located four miles out of Taylorsville, Kentucky, and continues to serve the folks in this area some of the best home-cooked, true Kentucky-style meals available anywhere. Pies are a specialty for owner Yvonne Patterson.*

### Filling

1 cup sugar

⅓ cup all-purpose flour

2 cups whole or 2 percent milk

3 egg yolks, beaten

3 tablespoons butter

1 teaspoon vanilla extract

1 cup flaked coconut

Prebaked 9-inch pie shell

### Meringue

3 egg whites

1 teaspoon cornstarch

3 tablespoons sugar

1 teaspoon vanilla extract

**To make filling,** combine sugar and flour. Mix well. Stir in milk and cook on low heat until thickened. Stir small amount of hot mixture into beaten egg yolks and add to hot mixture. Cook 2 or 3 minutes longer. Add butter, vanilla extract, and coconut. Pour into pie shell. Preheat oven to 350 degrees.

**To make meringue,** combine ingredients and beat until stiff. Spread meringue over pie, making sure edges are sealed. Bake until peaks of meringue are golden brown.

*Yield:* 8 servings

## ∞ EGG CUSTARD PIE ∞

*My grandmother, Loraine Beasy, taught me that a custard pie should be smooth as silk. This one is.*

1 (9-inch) pie shell, unbaked

4 eggs

2¼ cups whole milk

⅔ cup sugar

1½ teaspoons vanilla extract

¼ teaspoon salt

Ground nutmeg

Preheat oven to 400 degrees. Bake pie shell for 5 minutes. Cool on wire rack. Beat eggs in mixing bowl and add milk, sugar, vanilla extract, and salt. Continue beating on medium speed for 2½ to 3 minutes, or until well blended. Pour filling into pie shell. Sprinkle with nutmeg and bake for 15 minutes. Reduce heat to 325 degrees and continue baking for 35 to 40 minutes, or until knife inserted 1 inch from center comes out clean. Cool on wire rack.

*Yield:* 8 servings

# PEANUT BUTTER PIE

*Gambill Mansion Bed and Breakfast*

*Ella Seals operates Gambill Mansion Bed and Breakfast in Blaine, Kentucky. She pampers her guests with wonderful dishes and a personalized getaway.*

### Shell

1½ cups fine graham cracker crumbs

¼ pound (1 stick) margarine, melted

1 teaspoon sugar

### Filling

1 quart vanilla ice cream, softened

½ cup light corn syrup

⅓ cup creamy peanut butter

⅔ cup chopped, dry roasted, unsalted peanuts

Preheat oven to 350 degrees.

**To make shell,** combine graham cracker crumbs, melted margarine, and sugar. Press onto the bottom and sides of a 9-inch pie plate. Bake for 10 minutes. Refrigerate until chilled.

**To make filling,** press half of ice cream into shell. Stir corn syrup and peanut butter together in small bowl until well blended. Pour half of mixture over ice cream. Sprinkle with half of peanuts. Repeat layering. Freeze for about 5 hours.

*Yield:* 8 servings
*Note:* Let stand at room temperature for 5 minutes
for easy cutting.

# GERMAN SWEET CHOCOLATE PIE

1 (4-ounce) package German sweet chocolate

4 tablespoons (½ stick) butter

1 (13-ounce) can evaporated milk

1½ cups sugar

3 tablespoons cornstarch

⅛ teaspoon salt

2 eggs

1 teaspoon vanilla extract

1 (9-inch) pie shell, unbaked

1⅓ cups flaked coconut

½ cup chopped pecans

Preheat oven to 375 degrees.

Melt chocolate with butter over low heat. Stir until blended. Remove from heat and gradually blend in evaporated milk. Mix sugar, cornstarch, and salt thoroughly. Beat in eggs and vanilla extract. Gradually blend in chocolate mixture. Pour mixture into pie shell. Combine coconut and pecans and sprinkle over filling. Bake for 45 to 50 minutes, or until puffed and browned. Filling will be soft until completely cooled. Refrigerate at least 4 hours before cutting.

*Yield:* 8 servings
*Note:* If top browns too quickly while baking,
cover loosely with foil the last 15 minutes of baking.

# ❧ GREEN TOMATO PIE ❧

*A favorite way to use up those green tomatoes left over in the garden, this pie will surprise you with its unusual flavor.*

6 large green tomatoes

1 (9-inch) double-crust pie shell, unbaked

1 cup sugar

⅓ cup all-purpose flour

1 teaspoon ground cinnamon

½ teaspoon ground allspice

1½ tablespoons cider vinegar

2 tablespoons butter

Preheat oven to 400 degrees.

Cut tomatoes into ¼-inch-thick slices and place one-third of slices in pie shell. Mix sugar, flour, cinnamon, and allspice in large bowl and toss to mix. Cover first layer of tomatoes with one-third of sugar mixture. Repeat layering two more times, ending with sugar. Drizzle vinegar over top of pie and dot with butter. Cover with top crust, vent several times, and crimp to seal. Bake until juices are bubbling and crust is well browned, 35 to 45 minutes.

*Yield:* 8 servings

# Ꮼ LEMON MERINGUE PIE Ꮼ

### Filling

1 cup sugar

3 tablespoons cornstarch

1½ cups cold water

3 egg yolks

Grated rind of 1 lemon

¼ cup lemon juice

1 teaspoon butter or margarine

Prebaked 9-inch pie shell

### Meringue

3 egg whites

¼ cup sugar

Preheat oven to 350 degrees.

**To make filling,** stir together sugar and cornstarch in saucepan. Gradually stir in water until smooth. Add egg yolks and bring to a boil over medium heat, stirring constantly. Cook 1 minute longer and remove from heat. Stir in lemon rind, lemon juice, and butter. Cool. Pour into pie shell.

**To make meringue,** beat egg whites in small bowl until foamy. Gradually beat in sugar and continue beating until stiff peaks form. Spread meringue over pie, making sure edges are sealed. Bake until peaks of meringue are golden brown.

*Yield:* 8 servings

# MARGARITA PIE

### Shell

1½ cups fine pretzel crumbs

¼ pound (1 stick) butter or margarine, melted

1 tablespoon sugar

### Filling

1 envelope (1 tablespoon) unflavored gelatin

¼ cup water

4 eggs, separated

1 cup plus 2 tablespoons sugar

1 teaspoon grated lime peel

⅔ cup lime juice

2 tablespoons tequila

2 tablespoons orange-flavored liqueur

1 drop green food coloring

½ cup heavy whipping cream

Pretzels for garnish

Preheat oven to 375 degrees.

**To make shell,** combine pretzel crumbs, butter, and sugar in small bowl. Press mixture onto bottom and sides of 9-inch pie plate. Bake for 10 minutes, until lightly browned. Cool on wire rack.

**To make filling,** sprinkle gelatin over water in medium saucepan. Let stand for 5 minutes to soften slightly. Lightly beat egg yolks and stir into gelatin mixture with ½ cup of the sugar, lime peel, and lime juice. Cook over low heat, stirring constantly, until mixture thickens slightly and coats metal spoon, about 10 minutes. Stir in tequila, liqueur, and food coloring. Chill until mixture is consistency of unbeaten egg whites, about 45 minutes. In medium bowl, beat egg whites until foamy. Gradually beat in ½ cup of the sugar until stiff peaks form. Gently fold egg whites into gelatin mixture. Chill until mixture mounds slightly when dropped from spoon. Spoon into pie shell. Chill until firm, about 4 hours.

In medium bowl, beat cream and remaining 2 tablespoons sugar with electric mixer on high speed until stiff peaks form. Decorate pie with whipped cream and garnish with pretzels.

*Yield:* 8 servings

## ❧ EASY CHERRY COBBLER ❧

*I've met so many good Kentucky cooks who make cobbler this way when there's no time for the more time consuming rolled-out pastry cobbler. It's delicious with any type of fruit and proof positive that you can have dessert without a lot of fuss.*

5 tablespoons butter

¾ cup sugar

1 cup all-purpose flour

2 teaspoons baking powder

¼ teaspoon salt

¾ cup 2 percent milk

½ teaspoon almond extract

1 (16-ounce) can red sour pitted cherries with liquid

Preheat oven to 325 degrees. Melt butter in 9 x 9-inch glass dish. In mixing bowl, combine sugar, flour, baking powder, salt, and milk. Pour over melted butter. Do not stir together. Combine almond extract with cherries and liquid. Pour over batter. Do not stir together.

Bake until golden brown and bubbly, about 45 minutes. Top with vanilla ice cream while warm.

*Yield:* 6 servings

# ITALIAN CREAM CAKE

### Cake
¼ pound (1 stick) butter

½ cup solid vegetable shortening

2 cups sugar

5 eggs, separated

2 cups cake flour

1 teaspoon baking soda

1 cup buttermilk

1 teaspoon vanilla extract

1 cup flaked coconut

1 cup chopped pecans

### Frosting
1 (8-ounce) package cream cheese, softened

4 tablespoons (½ stick) butter, softened

3½ cups powdered sugar

1 teaspoon vanilla extract

Chopped pecans

Preheat oven to 350 degrees.

Cream butter and shortening. Add sugar and beat until smooth. Add egg yolks and beat well. Combine cake flour and baking soda. Add to creamed mixture alternately with buttermilk. Stir in vanilla extract. Add coconut and pecans. Beat egg whites until stiff and fold in. Pour into 3 greased and floured 8-inch cake pans. Bake for 25 minutes, or until toothpick comes out clean. Cool thoroughly and frost.

**To make frosting,** beat cream cheese and butter until smooth. Add powdered sugar and mix well. Add vanilla extract and beat until smooth. Spread between layers and on top and sides of cake. Sprinkle with pecans.

*Yield:* 12 servings

# THE CAKE

*My family calls this simply "The Cake!"*
*Once you taste it you will call it that, too.*

### Cake

4 cups fine graham cracker crumbs

2 cups sugar

½ pound (2 sticks) margarine, melted

4 eggs, beaten

1 teaspoon baking powder

1 cup whole or 2 percent milk

1 cup flaked coconut

1 cup chopped pecans

1 teaspoon vanilla extract

### Glaze

1 (15-ounce) can crushed pineapple with liquid

1 cup sugar

4 tablespoons all-purpose flour

Preheat oven to 350 degrees.

Combine graham cracker crumbs and sugar. Add margarine, then eggs. Add baking powder, milk, coconut, pecans, and vanilla extract, in that order. Mix well and pour into greased and floured 13 x 9 x 2-inch pan. Bake for 35 to 40 minutes.

**To make glaze,** combine all ingredients in saucepan and cook over medium heat until thick. Pour over warm cake.

*Yield:* 10 servings
*Note:* This cake tastes best after sitting at least 1 day.

# FRESH BANANA CAKE WITH BUTTER CREAM FROSTING

*Lorene Fulkerson*

*Lorene Fulkerson from Ohio County is one of the best Kentucky cooks I know. Her kitchen says "welcome" to anyone who walks through the door. Her fresh banana cake is excellent, and anyone fortunate enough to sit at her table will attest to her culinary talent.*

### Cake
4 eggs, beaten

3 cups sugar

1 cup solid vegetable shortening

5 large bananas, mashed

1 teaspoon vanilla extract

1 cup chopped nuts

4 cups all-purpose flour

1 teaspoon baking soda

1 cup buttermilk

### Frosting
About 8 cups powdered sugar

½ cup water

½ cup solid vegetable shortening

1 teaspoon vanilla extract

4 drops butter flavoring

Preheat oven to 350 degrees.

Cream eggs, sugar, and shortening. Add bananas and beat well. Add vanilla extract and nuts. Mix flour and baking soda and add buttermilk. Beat until well blended and add to egg mixture. Pour into 3 greased and floured 8-inch cake pans. Bake for 25 minutes, or until cake springs back when touched.

**To make frosting,** combine all ingredients and mix with electric mixer on high for 4 minutes. Spread between layers and on top and sides of cake.

*Yield:* 12 servings

# ✒ APPLE FARM CAKE ✒

¼ cup solid vegetable shortening

1 cup granulated sugar

1 egg

4 cups chopped apple (about 4 medium apples)

1 cup unsifted all-purpose flour

1 teaspoon baking soda

⅛ teaspoon salt

1 teaspoon ground cinnamon

½ teaspoon ground nutmeg

¼ teaspoon ground cloves

Powdered sugar

Preheat oven to 325 degrees.

Cream shortening and sugar. Mix in egg and apples. Sift together flour, baking soda, salt, cinnamon, nutmeg, and cloves. Add to apple mixture. Mix well. Batter will be thick. Spread in greased 9-inch-square baking pan. Bake for about 45 minutes, or until toothpick inserted in center comes out clean. While warm, cut into squares. Sprinkle with powdered sugar.

*Yield:* 9 servings

# WHITE CHOCOLATE CAKE
# WITH CREAM CHEESE ICING

### Cake

¾ pound (3 sticks) butter or margarine

2 cups sugar

4 eggs, separated

1 tablespoon vanilla extract

¼ pound white chocolate

2½ cups cake flour

1 teaspoon baking powder

1 cup buttermilk

½ cup pecans, chopped

1 cup flaked coconut

### Icing

¼ pound (1 stick) margarine, softened

6 ounces cream cheese, softened

3½ cups powdered sugar

½ cup pecans, chopped

Preheat oven to 325 degrees.

Melt chocolate in double boiler over hot water. Cream together butter and sugar. Beat in egg yolks one at a time. Add vanilla extract and chocolate. Sift together cake flour and baking powder. Add flour mixture, alternating with buttermilk, to creamed mixture. Beat egg whites until stiff and fold in. Add pecans and coconut. Pour into 3 greased and floured 8-inch cake pans and bake for 25 minutes. Cool before icing.

**To make icing,** cream together margarine, cream cheese, and powdered sugar. Add pecans. Spread between layers and on top and sides of cake.

*Yield:* 12 servings

# PRUNE CAKE WITH BUTTERMILK GLAZE

**Cake**

2 cups self-rising flour

1½ cups sugar

1 teaspoon ground cinnamon

1 teaspoon ground allspice

½ teaspoon ground nutmeg

3 eggs

¾ cup vegetable oil

1 cup buttermilk

1½ teaspoons vanilla extract

1 cup cooked prunes, puréed

¾ cup chopped pecans

**Glaze**

4 tablespoons (½ stick) butter

¾ cup sugar

½ cup buttermilk

1 tablespoon light corn syrup

1 teaspoon vanilla extract

Preheat oven to 325 degrees. Grease and flour 13 x 9 x 2-inch pan. Sift together self-rising flour, sugar, cinnamon, allspice, and nutmeg into large bowl. In separate bowl, beat eggs and stir in oil, buttermilk, and vanilla extract. Add egg mixture to dry ingredients, stirring only until blended. Add prunes and pecans and blend thoroughly. Pour into pan. Bake for 35 to 40 minutes, or until cake begins to pull from sides.

**To make glaze,** combine all ingredients in medium saucepan. Bring to a boil over medium heat. Stir constantly until butter is melted. Pour over hot cake. Cool in pan.

*Yield:* 10 servings

# FRESH COCONUT CAKE ❧ WITH WHITE FROSTING SUPREME

## Cake

½ pound (2 sticks) unsalted butter (no substitutions)

2 cups sugar

5 eggs

1 teaspoon baking soda

1 teaspoon baking powder

Dash of salt

2¾ cups cake flour

1 cup buttermilk

1 teaspoon vanilla extract

½ to ¾ teaspoon coconut flavoring

2 cups grated fresh coconut

## Frosting

½ cup water

2½ cups granulated sugar

3 tablespoons light corn syrup

3 egg whites

2½ tablespoons powdered sugar

Preheat oven to 350 degrees.

Cream butter and sugar until perfectly smooth, about 15 minutes on electric mixer. Add eggs, beating well after each addition. Sift baking soda, baking powder, salt, and cake flour together and add to creamed mixture alternately with buttermilk. Stir in vanilla extract and coconut flavoring. Pour into 3 greased and floured 9-inch pans. Bake for about 25 minutes, or until a toothpick inserted comes out clean. Cool before frosting.

**To make frosting,** mix water, granulated sugar, and corn syrup in large saucepan. Bring slowly to a boil over medium heat, stirring constantly, until sugar is dissolved. Cook to 235 degrees on candy thermometer, or to soft ball stage, without stirring.

While syrup is cooking, beat egg whites with electric mixer until stiff but not dry. Slowly add syrup to beaten whites, continuing to beat as you pour. Beat until mixture is consistency of whipped cream. Add powdered sugar and beat until well blended.

Spread frosting and sprinkle coconut on each layer and on sides of cake.

*Yield:* 10 to 12 servings

## ➆ BAVARIAN CREAM ➆ FOR FRESH FRUIT

2 envelopes (2 tablespoons) unflavored gelatin

1¼ cups water

1¼ cups whole milk

2 eggs, well beaten

1 cup sugar

1 teaspoon vanilla extract

3 cups light whipping cream, whipped

In small saucepan sprinkle gelatin over 1¼ cups water and cook over low heat, stirring constantly, until gelatin dissolves, about 3 minutes. Remove from heat.

In top of double boiler, combine milk, eggs, and sugar. Cook, stirring often, until mixture thickens and coats a spoon. Remove from heat. Add gelatin and vanilla extract. Cool.

Rinse 2-quart mold with cold water. Fold whipped cream into milk mixture and pour into mold. Refrigerate until set. Unmold and serve immediately with fresh fruit.

*Yield:* 8 servings

# CRÈME ANGLAISE

*Crème Anglaise is a light custard sauce that is excellent over fruit or ice cream.*

4 egg yolks
¼ cup sugar
1 tablespoon cornstarch
2 cups whole or 2 percent milk
1 teaspoon vanilla extract

Beat egg yolks and sugar until mixture forms ribbons when lifted above bowl. In top of double boiler dissolve cornstarch in milk and cook over medium heat until bubbles begin to form. Add egg yolk mixture and whisk until thick. Remove from heat and add vanilla extract. Place pan on ice and continue stirring until cooled. Cover.

*Yield:* 2½ cups

# FRESH STRAWBERRY SAUCE

2 cups fresh strawberries, sliced
2 tablespoons sugar
1½ teaspoons cornstarch
¼ teaspoon almond extract

Combine strawberries and sugar. Cover and refrigerate for several hours. Drain strawberries, reserving juice. Set strawberries aside. Add enough water to strawberry juice to make ½ cup. Combine juice and cornstarch in saucepan and stir until cornstarch is dissolved. Cook over medium heat, stirring constantly, until smooth and thick. Stir in strawberries and almond extract. Chill.

*Yield:* 1¼ cups
*Note:* Serve this sauce over slices of angel food or pound cake. It's also great over ice cream or pancakes.

# BOURBON SAUCE

*Rebecca-Ruth Candies*

*Anyone who knows Kentucky knows that we Kentuckians wrote the book on bourbon candy making, and no one does it better than Rebecca-Ruth Candies, who says this of its wonderful sauce: "This makes a great sauce for vanilla ice cream, pound cake, cheesecake, or any other dessert. It is particularly well suited for desserts with subtle flavor. This way your guests who are more adventurous can go crazy. When served with a dessert that is white or cream in color, the sauce can be artistically added to create contrast, thus providing the ambiance required for a fine dessert. In the past a double boiler was used to make this sauce. Nowadays this dessert sauce is very simple to make in the microwave. In the microwave it takes only a few minutes and produces a sauce that is far better than any sauce that is available on a commercial basis."*

16 Rebecca-Ruth Candies bourbon balls

¼ cup whole milk

Place bourbon balls in microwave-safe bowl and add milk. Microwave at High for 1 to 2 minutes, until chocolate can be mushed with spoon. (Do not let milk boil over.) Mix well and serve.

*Yield:* 4 servings as a sauce

# ∽ DELUXE LEMON BARS ∽

2 cups sifted all-purpose flour

½ cup powdered sugar

½ pound (2 sticks) butter (no substitutions)

4 eggs, beaten

2 cups granulated sugar

1 teaspoon grated lemon zest

⅓ cup lemon juice

¼ cup all-purpose flour

½ teaspoon baking powder

Preheat oven to 350 degrees.

Sift together 2 cups flour and powdered sugar. Cut in butter until mixture clings together. Press into 13 x 9 x 2-inch baking pan. Bake for 20 to 25 minutes, until lightly browned. Beat together eggs, granulated sugar, lemon zest, and lemon juice. Sift together ¼ cup flour and baking powder. Stir into egg mixture. Pour over baked crust. Bake for 25 more minutes. Sprinkle with additional powdered sugar. Cool. Cut into bars.

*Yield:* 30 servings

# NUT BARS

### Crust
1 cup all-purpose flour
¼ pound (1 stick) butter, softened

### Filling
2 eggs
1½ cups light brown sugar
¾ cup flaked coconut
1 cup chopped pecans
2 tablespoons all-purpose flour
¼ teaspoon baking powder
½ teaspoon salt
1½ teaspoons vanilla extract

### Icing
2 tablespoons butter
1½ cups powdered sugar
3 tablespoons orange juice
1 teaspoon lemon juice
1 teaspoon grated lemon zest

Preheat oven to 350 degrees.

**To make crust,** blend together flour and butter until crumbly. Press onto bottom and sides of a 9-inch-square pan and bake for 15 minutes.

**To make filling,** beat ingredients until well mixed and pour over crust. Bake for 20 more minutes. Cool.

**To make icing,** beat ingredients until creamy and spread on top. Sprinkle with chopped pecans and cut into squares.

*Yield:* 16 squares

# ❧ BREAD PUDDING ❧
## WITH VANILLA SAUCE

*No matter what type of potluck I go to, someone always asks*
*if I brought my bread pudding. This is comfort food at its best.*

### Pudding
½ loaf white bread

1 cup sugar

4 eggs

2 cups half-and-half

¼ pound (1 stick) butter, melted

½ teaspoon salt

1 teaspoon vanilla extract

### Vanilla Sauce
1 cup water

1 cup sugar

2 tablespoons cornstarch

⅛ teaspoon salt

2 tablespoons butter

1 teaspoon vanilla extract

Preheat oven to 350 degrees.

Tear bread into chunks and place in buttered 2-quart casserole. Beat sugar and eggs until light and fluffy. Add milk, butter, salt, and vanilla extract. Pour over bread. Bake for 35 to 40 minutes, until browned and top puffs.

**To make vanilla sauce,** heat water, sugar, cornstarch, and salt in medium saucepan until slightly thickened. Remove from heat and add butter and vanilla extract. Spoon over servings of warm bread pudding.

*Yield:* 8 servings

# MY FAVORITE BANANA PUDDING

*There are many recipes for banana puddings, some using instant pudding or pudding mix and others using food coloring. This is my favorite and is certainly worth the effort of making "from scratch." My Scotty always calls it "THE pudding."*

1 cup plus 2 tablespoons sugar

⅓ cup all-purpose flour

¼ teaspoon salt

4 eggs, separated

2¼ cups whole or 2 percent milk

2 tablespoons unsalted butter

1 teaspoon vanilla extract

1 (12-ounce) box vanilla wafers

5 ripe bananas, sliced

Fine vanilla wafer crumbs

Preheat oven to 425 degrees.

Mix 1 cup sugar, flour, and salt in heavy saucepan. Beat egg yolks with milk and add to flour mixture. Cook over medium heat, stirring constantly. Reduce heat after mixture begins to thicken. Continue stirring until very thick. Remove from heat and add butter and vanilla extract.

Line 2-quart baking dish with vanilla wafers on bottom and sides. Add one-third of banana slices to cover wafers. Pour one-third of pudding mixture over bananas. Repeat layering two more times.

Beat egg whites with the 2 tablespoons sugar until stiff; spread over pudding. Sprinkle wafer crumbs over top and brown lightly in oven.

*Yield:* 8 servings

# ✇ BUTTERSCOTCH MOUSSE ✇

8 ounces butterscotch morsels

3 tablespoons powdered sugar

2 tablespoons strong brewed coffee

3 egg yolks

1 (8-ounce) tub whipped topping, thawed

Melt butterscotch morsels over medium heat in double boiler. Remove top pan from heat and add powdered sugar and coffee. Stir well. Add 1 egg yolk at a time, stirring until smooth.

Place top pan back over boiling water. Cook, stirring constantly, for 3 to 4 minutes, until thickened.

Pour into bowl. Chill for 6 to 8 minutes and fold in 3 cups of the whipped topping. Spoon into dishes. Top with remaining whipped topping.

*Yield:* 4 servings

# CARAMEL FLAN

1 cup sugar

2 cups half-and-half

1 cup whole milk

2 teaspoons vanilla extract

6 eggs

2 egg yolks

Preheat oven to 325 degrees. Heat 6-cup ring mold in oven for 8 to 10 minutes, or until hot.

Heat ½ cup of the sugar in heavy skillet over medium-high heat for 5 to 7 minutes, or until sugar is completely melted and amber colored. Stir frequently, taking care not to burn. Immediately pour caramelized sugar into ring mold, holding mold with mitten. Rotate quickly to coat bottom and sides evenly with caramelized sugar. Place mold on wire rack to cool.

Combine half-and-half and milk in heavy 2-quart pan. Heat over medium heat until liquid almost simmers. Remove and add the remaining ½ cup sugar and vanilla extract, stirring until sugar dissolves.

Beat eggs and egg yolks together until well blended. Gradually stir in milk mixture. Pour into ring mold. Place mold in large pan and pour hot water into pan coming up ½ inch on sides. Bake for 35 to 40 minutes, or until knife inserted into center of custard comes out clean. Remove from water bath and place on wire rack. Allow to cool for 30 minutes.

Cover mold and refrigerate for 2 hours, until thoroughly chilled. To serve, loosen inner and outer edges of flan with knife. Cover mold with rimmed plate and invert. Lift off mold and spoon remaining caramel from mold over flan.

*Yield:* 8 servings

# CHARLOTTE RUSSE

24 ladyfingers, split

2 envelopes (2 tablespoons) unflavored gelatin

2 cups milk (2 percent, whole, or evaporated)

2 teaspoons vanilla extract

4 cups heavy whipping cream

1½ cups granulated sugar

1 cup heavy whipping cream, whipped

1 tablespoon powdered sugar

Chocolate curls for garnish (see note)

Line bottom and sides of truffle bowl with ladyfingers. Mix gelatin and milk and heat over medium heat until gelatin dissolves.

Remove from heat and add vanilla extract. Whip 4 cups whipping cream, gradually adding granulated sugar. Fold into cooled gelatin mixture. Pour gently into truffle bowl, being careful not to move ladyfingers. Refrigerate until set.

Sweeten whipped cream with powdered sugar and lightly spread over top. Garnish with chocolate curls.

*Yield:* 10 to 12 servings

*Note:* Make chocolate curls out of a good-quality chocolate bar by refrigerating bar for about 10 minutes and "shaving" it with vegetable peeler.

# CHOCOLATE ELEGANCE

⅓ cups semisweet chocolate chips
½ pound (2 sticks) unsalted butter
4 tablespoons superfine sugar
5 large eggs, separated
2 tablespoons Tia Maria liqueur
Chocolate curls for garnish (see note)

Combine chocolate pieces, butter, and 3 tablespoons of the sugar. Cook in top of double boiler over medium heat until chocolate melts. Beat egg yolks slightly. Slowly add chocolate mixture to yolks and beat on high speed with electric mixer for 10 minutes.

Beat egg whites until stiff, adding remaining 1 tablespoon sugar gradually. Add beaten egg whites to chocolate mixture along with liqueur. Beat on high speed another 10 minutes.

Pour into buttered 2-quart soufflé dish and refrigerate for 10 to 12 hours. Unmold 2 hours before serving by dipping bottom and sides of dish into hot water. Run knife around sides of dish to loosen. Invert dish onto serving plate and smooth surface with knife. Decorate with chocolate curls. Refrigerate until serving time.

*Yield:* 12 servings
*Note:* Make chocolate curls out of a good-quality chocolate bar by refrigerating bar for about 10 minutes and "shaving" with vegetable peeler.

# CARAMELS

*When I first began writing for* Kentucky Living, *I invited readers to send me recipes. Garnett Doyle of Clarkson, Kentucky, was the first to submit some of his favorites. One of my favorites is his recipe for Caramels.*

1 (14-ounce) can sweetened condensed milk

¼ pound (1 stick) butter or margarine

2 cups sugar

1 (16-ounce) bottle light corn syrup

Pinch of salt (optional)

1 teaspoon vanilla extract

Nuts (optional)

Before starting, butter cookie pan (minimum size 10 inches wide by 16 inches long by 1 inch deep). Open can of condensed milk. Once mixture is boiling, you must stir constantly and won't have time to do these things.

In a heavy saucepan mix together butter, sugar, corn syrup, and salt (if using) and bring to a boil. After mixture comes to a boil, add condensed milk, stirring constantly. Cook until soft ball is formed in water. The best way to do this is to cook to 235 degrees on candy thermometer. Remove from heat and when boiling stops, stir in vanilla extract. If you want nuts in the candy, add them at this time.

Pour mixture into buttered cookie pan and let cool. Cut and wrap pieces in waxed paper.

*Yield:* 2 to 3 dozen, depending on how cut

# ❧ SOPAIPILLAS ❧

*"Soap-a-pee-yas" are a traditional Mexican dessert.*

1¾ cups sifted all-purpose flour

2 teaspoons baking powder

1 teaspoon salt

2 tablespoons solid vegetable shortening

⅔ cup cold water

Vegetable oil for frying

Heat 1 inch oil in a heavy skillet over medium heat.

Combine flour, baking powder, and salt. Sift into mixing bowl. Cut in shortening with pastry blender. Add enough water to make a stiff dough. Turn dough onto lightly floured board and knead lightly until smooth. Cover with clean dish towel and let rest 10 minutes.

Roll dough very thin (about ⅛ inch thick) into rectangle about 15 inches by 12 inches. Cut into 2-inch squares.

When oil is very hot, drop a few squares of dough into it at a time. Turn frequently so that sopaipillas will puff up evenly. Remove from oil with slotted spoon. Drain on paper towels. Serve hot with powdered sugar or honey.

*Yield:* 6 servings

# SWEET POTATO CHIPS

Claudia Sanders Dinner House of Shelbyville, Kentucky,
Cookbook *by Cherry Settles, Tommy Settles, and Edward G. Klemm*

1½ quarts cooking oil
3 large sweet potatoes, peeled and thinly sliced
Powdered sugar

Heat cooking oil in large pot over high heat (to 350 degrees, if using cooking thermometer). Soak sweet potato slices in cold water for 10 minutes. Drain slices on paper towels. Drop slices in oil and fry until lightly browned. Remove from oil with slotted spoon and drain on paper towels. Sprinkle with powdered sugar.

*Yield:* 6 servings

# PEANUT BUTTER TREATS

4 cups Special K cereal
1 cup sugar
1 cup light corn syrup
1 cup creamy peanut butter

Put cereal in large mixing bowl. Combine sugar and syrup in saucepan. Stir together over medium heat until sugar dissolves. Remove from heat and stir in peanut butter. When blended, pour over cereal. Stir quickly to coat cereal and drop by tablespoonfuls onto waxed paper.

*Yield:* 20 servings
*Note:* This is an excellent quick treat to make for kids.
It also packs well in lunches.

# RANGER COOKIES

½ cup granulated sugar

½ cup butter-flavored solid vegetable shortening

1 egg

½ teaspoon vanilla extract

½ teaspoon baking soda

¼ teaspoon salt

1 cup puffed-rice cereal

1 cup pecans, chopped

½ cup light brown sugar (packed)

1 cup all-purpose flour

¼ teaspoon baking powder

1 cup oats (3-minute variety)

½ cup flaked coconut

Preheat oven to 350 degrees.

Cream granulated sugar and shortening. Add egg and beat well. Add all other ingredients and blend together. Batter will be very thick. Dip out batter by teaspoonfuls. Roll each into a small ball. Place on cookie sheet and press down with fingers. Bake for 10 minutes.

*Yield:* 3 dozen cookies

# Derby Favorites

# Derby Favorites

 My memories of Derby time when I was young are
wonderful. One occasion wasn't so pleasant, though.
My mother and my grandmother ironed bed linens,
tablecloths, and napkins on a huge electric ironer in
the basement of my grandparents' old home. At
Derby time they would spend days preparing for
company by polishing, cleaning, and ironing. I
remember how big that ironer looked to me when I
was very small and the smell that it made as it per-
formed its task.

"What's wrong?" I recall my grandmother asking
me as I sat next to her, stacking napkins. She sensed
how concerned this five-year-old was about some-
thing.

"Derby's gonna smell awful, Nannan," I told her,
mistaking the smell of the ironer for the Derby
desserts baking upstairs in the oven. "Derby's gonna
smell awful."

Horses are part of my soul, and memories of the Kentucky Derby are among my favorites. Derby foods are always a part of those memories. I grew up in a family where horses and the Kentucky Derby were quite the traditions. My father, Harold Allison, broke wild horses with his brother, Raymond, in their native Montana. He astounded my mother on their honeymoon in Great Falls by leading her horse out of quicksand. As a child, I loved the stories of these true bronco busters.

I remember my grandparents often having out-of-town guests for the Kentucky Derby and the fuss that would be made over preparations for that first Saturday in May.

I have celebrated the Derby in many states, always getting teary eyed when "My Old Kentucky Home" was played on the television and always wishing I was home for that very special day. Our Derby parties over the years have evolved from large gatherings with televisions set outside and elaborate buffets to small gatherings of family and friends.

I have collected many recipes over the years, and I still love to cook at Derby time. I feature here Bacon and Cheese Spoon Bread, which has a great texture, and Wild Turkey Racehorse Pie, made with our own great Kentucky bourbon. The Kurtz Restaurant's Biscuit Pudding with Jim Beam Bourbon Sauce is in itself a celebration of Kentucky cuisine.

Whether your Derby gathering consists of a few or many, these recipes are sure to delight your guests. Make a statement in May.

# PEACH-CARAMEL FRENCH TOAST

*Jailer's Inn Bed and Breakfast*

1 (29-ounce) can sliced peaches with syrup

1½ cup granulated sugar

¼ pound (1 stick) margarine

1 cup light brown sugar

2 tablespoons water

6 slices white bread

5 eggs

1¼ cups milk

1 tablespoon vanilla extract

Drain peaches and reserve syrup. Heat granulated sugar and margarine in microwave at High for 1 minute. Add brown sugar and microwave for 1 more minute. Add water and continue microwaving until thick and foamy, 1 to 2 minutes. Pour into 13 x 9 x 2-inch baking dish and cool for 10 minutes.

Place peaches on cooled caramel sauce and cover with slices of bread placed close together. Beat eggs, milk, and vanilla extract until mixed. Pour over bread, cover, and refrigerate overnight.

Preheat oven to 350 degrees and bake for 40 minutes. Loosely cover with foil for last 10 minutes if browning too fast. Serve with warmed peach syrup.

*Yield:* 12 to 14 servings

# KENTUCKY GLAZED CANADIAN BACON

3 pounds Canadian bacon

½ cup light brown sugar

1 tablespoon flour

½ teaspoon dry mustard

Dash of ground cloves

2 tablespoons water

Preheat oven to 350 degrees.

Remove casing from bacon, if necessary. Place bacon in baking pan and bake uncovered for 1½ hours. Combine brown sugar, flour, mustard, and cloves. Mix well. Stir in water and brush half of mixture over bacon. Bake for 10 more minutes. Brush with remaining glaze and bake an additional 5 minutes.

*Yield:* 12 to 14 servings

*Note:* This is an excellent brunch dish served with eggs.

# PUMPKIN WAFFLES

*Pineapple Inn Bed and Breakfast*

*Take my word for it—these are worth the effort!*

2 cups flour

2 tablespoons baking powder

1 tablespoon ground cinnamon

½ teaspoon ground coriander

½ teaspoon ground nutmeg or mace

½ teaspoon salt

4 egg yolks

1½ cups milk (not fat-free)

1 cup cooked or canned pumpkin

1½ sticks butter or margarine, melted

1 tablespoon vanilla extract

4 egg whites

Combine flour, baking powder, cinnamon, coriander, nutmeg, and salt. Beat egg yolks slightly and beat in milk, pumpkin, butter, and vanilla extract. Add pumpkin mixture to flour mixture, stirring just until combined but slightly lumpy. Beat egg whites until stiff peaks form. Gently fold into pumpkin mixture. Do not overmix.

Pour 1 to 1¼ cups batter onto grids of preheated, lightly greased waffle baker. Close lid. Do not open during baking. Bake according to manufacturer's directions. Repeat with remaining batter.

*Yield:* Six 9-inch waffles

## ☙ MY DERBY GRITS ☙

1 quart 2 percent milk

¼ pound (1 stick) unsalted butter

1 cup 3-minute grits

4 ounces Swiss or Gruyère cheese, grated (1 cup)

Salt and freshly ground pepper

1 ounce Parmesan cheese, grated (¼ cup)

Preheat oven to 375 degrees.

Bring milk and butter to a slow boil and stir in grits slowly. Stir often until mixture thickens. Put in large bowl and beat with electric mixer until grits become creamy, 5 to 7 minutes. Add grated cheese and salt and pepper. Mix well and pour into greased 2-quart casserole.

Put dots of butter on top and sprinkle with Parmesan cheese. Bake for 30 to 35 minutes.

*Yield:* 6 to 8 servings

# RED-EYE GRAVY FOR GRITS

1 cup strong brewed coffee
2 tablespoons drippings from fried country ham

Add coffee to drippings and bring to a boil. Reduce heat and simmer for 5 minutes. Serve over grits.

*Yield:* Enough for 6 to 8 servings of "My Derby Grits"

# OAKS CHEESE GRITS

*Maker's Mark Distillery*
*From* That Special Touch *by Sandra Davis*

*Each year at the popular Maker's Mark Distillery, Loretto, Kentucky, a fabulous Derby Oaks Brunch is catered by the very talented Mary Jane Shockency. Her tradition of fine Kentucky cooking is unequaled.*

2 cups boiling water
1⅓ cups instant grits
6 ounces cheddar cheese, grated (1½ cups, packed)
¼ cup Parmesan cheese
2 eggs, well beaten
2 tablespoons dried chives
Paprika for garnish

Preheat oven to 350 degrees and grease an 12 x 8 x 2-inch baking dish. Pour boiling water over grits, stirring until blended. Add cheeses, mixing thoroughly, until all cheeses are melted. Blend in eggs and chives. Pour into greased baking dish, sprinkle paprika on top, and bake 40 minutes, or until knife inserted into center comes out clean.

*Yield:* 6 servings

# BEATEN BISCUITS

*Cissy Gregg,* Louisville Courier-Journal

½ teaspoon salt

2 cups sifted flour

1 tablespoon lard

Ice water or chilled milk, using as little as possible

Add salt to flour and rub in the lard with the hands. Add the iced liquid—either water or milk, or equal parts of each—to make a stiff dough, kneading all the time. I don't have a kneader, but use elbow strength aided with a wooden mallet, which serves otherwise as an ice crusher, and a wooden board underneath the dough. Some people put the dough in a clean cloth, but I don't. Beat until the air is lively with snappings and crackings, and there are blisters on the dough. Cut into small biscuits, place on an ungreased baking sheet, pricked according to fashion, and bake in a 350 degree oven for 35 to 40 minutes.

*Yield:* 2 dozen

# BACON AND CHEESE SPOON BREAD

*Spoon bread is so very Kentucky, and this version is wonderful.
Add a fresh green salad and you have a great lunch!*

¾ cup cornmeal

1½ cups cold water

½ pound mild cheddar cheese, grated (2 cups)

4 tablespoons (½ stick) butter, softened

2 cloves garlic, minced

½ teaspoon salt

Dash of white pepper

1 cup whole milk

6 egg yolks, well beaten

½ pound sliced bacon, cooked crisp and crumbled

5 egg whites, stiffly beaten

Preheat oven to 325 degrees.

Combine cornmeal and water. Cook and stir until thick as mush. Remove from heat and add cheese, butter, garlic, salt, and white pepper. Stir to melt cheese. Gradually add milk and stir in egg yolks. Add bacon, reserving some for garnish. Fold in egg whites. Pour mixture into greased 2-quart casserole. Bake for 1 hour, or until golden brown. Top with butter and bacon crumbs.

*Yield:* 6 servings

# BANANA SALAD ✎

*Moonlite Bar-B-Q Inn*

*The Moonlite Bar-B-Q Inn of Owensboro, Kentucky, is truly a Kentucky tradition. The tradition of fine barbecue in this part of the state is known far and wide. And while I can't get the secret to its great-tasting barbecue sauce, I can feature the following recipe.*

### Dressing
1 egg yolk, beaten
½ cup sugar
2 tablespoons distilled white vinegar
½ cup light cream or Miracle Whip

### Banana Salad
12 bananas, peeled
1 cup crushed peanuts

**To make dressing,** mix egg yolk, sugar, and vinegar. Bring to a boil, stirring constantly since it sticks easily. Remove from heat and slowly add cream. Chill before using.

**To make salad,** slice 4 bananas ⅛ inch thick into bowl. Cover bananas with light layer of dressing. Sprinkle with layer of peanuts. Repeat layers until all bananas are used.

*Yield:* 12 servings

# COCHELLE SALAD

*Kitty Ellis operates Kathryn's Coordinating in Henderson, Kentucky,
and specializes in a three-foot-tall fruit tower served on giant silver
trays separated by cherubs. Kitty travels all over Kentucky
and Evansville, Indiana, catering and coordinating everything
from her beautiful wedding flowers to honeymoon arrangements.
Here is her show-stopping Cochelle Salad.*

### Salad

Fruit preservative to keep apples and bananas from turning

10 apples (any variety), peeled, cored, and chopped

10 navel oranges, peeled and sectioned

2 quarts fresh strawberries, capped and sliced in half

4 or 5 heads iceberg lettuce, shredded

3 cups peeled and grated carrots

3 cups chopped celery

10 bananas (just turning yellow)

2 to 3 cups broken pecan pieces

5 cups cherry tomatoes, halved

### Dressing

3 cups mayonnaise

1¼ cups light whipping cream

½ cup prepared mustard

1 teaspoon celery seed

Mix fruit preservative according to directions on package. Let apples
stand appropriate amount of time in solution. Remove and drain. Bananas should wait until last moments. Combine apples, oranges, and
strawberries in large container. Cover and chill. Combine lettuce, carrots, and celery. Cover and chill. Slice bananas; toss with fruit and set
aside. Transfer lettuce mixture to serving platter. Arrange fruit mixture
evenly over lettuce mixture. Add pecans and tomatoes.

**To make dressing,** blend mayonnaise, whipping cream, mustard, and celery seed well. Pour dressing over salad mixture and gently toss to coat.

*Yield:* 30 to 40 servings
*Note:* Fat-free mayonnaise and 2 percent milk can be substituted for the mayonnaise and whipping cream.

## ❧ VIDALIA ONION CASSEROLE ❧

*Margaret Trusty*

3 cups crushed round buttery crackers
¾ pound (3 sticks) margarine, melted
6 cups very thinly sliced Vidalia onions (5 or 6 large)
6 tablespoons (¾ stick) butter
1 clove garlic, chopped
6 eggs, beaten
2½ cups milk, warmed
2½ teaspoons salt
Dash of Tabasco
¼ teaspoon pepper
1½ teaspoons prepared mustard
1½ teaspoons Worcestershire sauce
6 ounces Parmesan cheese (1½ cups)
12 ounces Swiss cheese, grated (3 cups)
Paprika

Preheat oven to 350 degrees. To make crust, combine crushed crackers with melted margarine and press into large casserole. Layer onions over crust. Pour butter, garlic, eggs, milk, salt, Tabasco, pepper, mustard, Worcestershire sauce, and Parmesan cheese over onions. Bake for 20 to 30 minutes. Sprinkle Swiss cheese over mixture for last 10 minutes of baking. Sprinkle paprika on top.

*Yield:* 25 servings

# WILD TURKEY BOURBON MARINADE STEAK SAUCE

*Wild Turkey Distillery*

2 cups soy sauce

¼ cup Wild Turkey bourbon

2 tablespoons sugar

2 tablespoons dry mustard
2 tablespoons finely chopped ginger root
(or 1 tablespoon ground ginger)

1 tablespoon garlic salt

1 teaspoon Tabasco

Combine all ingredients and mix well. Pour into quart jar.

*Yield:* 1 quart

*Note:* Use this sauce to marinate red meats before cooking and to baste meats while cooking.

# HENRY BAIN SAUCE (MY WAY)

*I've come to the conclusion that it would be easier to get oranges out of a turnip than to get the Pendennis Club in Louisville, Kentucky, to give out its secret recipe for Henry Bain sauce. That's the famous sauce you know, created by Mr. Bain himself when he worked as head waiter for the club. I myself bargained, begged, and eventually got nowhere in my quest for this famous sauce's recipe. It has been sought after for so many years you'd think we'd all give up by now. I've come up with a recipe that's close—very close—and makes just about anything from steak fries to club crackers topped with cream cheese taste great. Just use a good chutney. I also feature below the chutney recipe I use for this copy of a fine Kentucky tradition. I wonder if Mr. Bain ever expected all this attention.*

1 (12-ounce) bottle chili sauce
1 (14-ounce) bottle ketchup
1 (11-ounce) bottle A-1 sauce
1 (10-ounce) bottle Worcestershire sauce
1 pint of my favorite chutney (recipe follows)
2 tablespoons Tabasco

Combine all ingredients and mix well. Store in pint jars in refrigerator.

## ⬦ CHUTNEY ⬦

1 pint cider vinegar
6 medium onions, chopped
2½ cups sugar
4 teaspoons salt
5 tablespoons ground ginger (packed)
4 hot peppers, chopped
3 pounds apples, peeled, cored, and chopped
½ pound chopped raisins

Boil vinegar, onions, sugar, salt, ginger, and peppers until almost the consistency of syrup. Add apples and cook over medium heat for 20 to 25 minutes, stirring constantly. When mixture begins to thicken, add raisins. Put in sterilized jars and seal.

*Yield:* 4 to 6 pints

# KENTUCKY COLONELS' BURGOO

*The Kentucky Colonels*

*This recipe is served by the Honorable Order of Kentucky Colonels at their annual Derby barbecue, held each year on the day after the Kentucky Derby on the grounds of Wickland Estate in historic Bardstown, Kentucky. Billie Hurst, Philip Lyvers, and Tony Lyvers are known as the Burgoo Kings in Kentucky.*

*According to the legend of the burgoo, the dish is to cook and simmer for twenty-four hours prior to being served. Burgoo chefs say that in preparing the burgoo the mysterious ingredient that is said to bring it all together is added sometime in the dark of the night. The chefs listen for and always hear a splatter in one of the pots. It is said that a big old black snake falls out of a tree into the pot. No one knows for sure whether this is true, but, like the legend of Sleepy Hollow, the tale has been passed down through the generations.*

8 pounds pork

1 pound veal

6 pounds breast of lamb

30 pounds beef

20 pounds chicken

20 pounds turtle meat

1½ gallons tomato purée

1 pound barley

1 gallon cut white corn

1 gallon whole cranberries

1 gallon chopped small mushrooms

1 gallon diced turnips

3 pounds Irish potatoes

10 pounds onions, chopped

20 green peppers

1 gallon sliced carrots

5 pounds cabbage

1 gallon chopped okra

1 gallon diced celery

3 tablespoons pepper

2 cups salt

6 ounces horseradish roots, finely grated

¼ cup Worcestershire sauce

3 tablespoons Italian-style seasoning

1 cup chopped fresh parsley

1½ tablespoons bay leaves

10 pods red pepper (well pulverized)

1½ tablespoons oregano

3 tablespoons chili seasoning

At noon on Saturday, the day before burgoo is to be served, cook meat in huge kettles over open fire, simmering for hours. Sunday morning, divide meat and mix it together in 6 or 7 huge kettles. Add vegetables and seasonings and cook them with meat, simmering about 4 hours.

*Yield:* 150 servings
*Note:* Any leftovers may be frozen.

# BURGOO

*Moonlite Bar-B-Q Inn*

4 pounds mutton

⅓ pound chicken

5 pounds potatoes, peeled and diced

¾ pound cabbage, ground or chopped fine

¾ pound onions, ground or chopped fine

2 (15-ounce) cans corn (we like shoe peg) or 2 cups fresh corn

¾ cup ketchup

Juice of 1 lemon (about 3 tablespoons)

2½ tablespoons salt (more if you like)

2 tablespoons black pepper

½ cup Worcestershire sauce

¾ cup distilled white vinegar

3 (10¾-ounce) cans tomato purée

1 teaspoon cayenne (more if you like)

Boil mutton in enough water to cover. Cook until tender, 2 to 3 hours. Throw out stock and bones. Chop meat fine. Set aside. Boil chicken in 2 gallons of water in large kettle until tender. Remove chicken and add potatoes, cabbage, onions, corn, ketchup, and 1 gallon of water to chicken stock. Bring to a boil.

Meanwhile, chop chicken meat and discard bones and skin. When potatoes are tender, add chicken, mutton, lemon juice, salt, black pepper, Worcestershire sauce, vinegar, tomato purée, and cayenne. Let this simmer for 2 hours or longer, stirring occasionally as it thickens.

*Yield:* 3 gallons

*Note:* Some area cooks add dried lima beans, tomatoes, and a little boiled shredded beef or wild game.

# PORK LOIN FOR FIFTY

*Margaret Trusty Catering*

*Margaret Trusty is a very talented caterer who lives in Mount Sterling, Kentucky. I found her in* Taste of Home *magazine and featured her in* Kentucky Living.

Preheat oven to 325 degrees. Rub a large whole boneless pork loin with dry mustard, thyme, rosemary, salt, pepper, and garlic. Place in large oven bag with ¼ cup water. Bake for about 2 hours at 325 degrees. Slice thin and serve with party bread or yeast rolls and your favorite mustard.

# ❧ SPECIAL MINT JULEP ❧

*Maker's Mark Distillery*
*From* That Special Touch *by Sandra Davis*

*"Bill Samuels (of Maker's Mark) believes three things can go wrong in making a perfect mint julep. The first is using a low-grade bourbon that has a strong, hot bite. The next mistake is using too much mint to cover up the bourbon's strong bite. The last is an over-infusion of sugar to cover up the mint. Try this special mint julep."*
—*Sandra Davis,* That Special Touch

Fresh mint

1 bottle Maker's Mark 90 proof bourbon

Granulated sugar

Water, preferably distilled

Mint sprigs and powdered sugar for garnish (optional)

To prepare mint extract, pick mint and remove leaves smaller than a dime. Wash, pat dry, put 40 leaves in mixing bowl, and cover with 3 ounces of Maker's Mark. Allow leaves to soak in bourbon for 15 minutes. Gather leaves in bundle. Put in clean cotton cloth and wring vigorously over bowl where leaves soaked—bruising leaves. Keep dipping in bourbon (several times) and wringing leaves so juice of mint is dripped back into bourbon. Let this mint extract sit.

FOR SIMPLE SYRUP, mix equal amounts of granulated sugar and water into cooking pot (example: 1 cup sugar and 1 cup water). Heat long enough for sugar to dissolve in water. Stir so sugar doesn't burn. Remove from heat and let cool. This can be done several hours in advance.

FOR JULEP MIXTURE, pour 3½ parts of Maker's Mark to 1 part simple syrup into large bowl. Begin adding mint extract in small portions. You must taste and smell—there is no formula since each extract will vary in strength. Pour finished julep stock into covered jar and refrigerate at least 24 hours to "marry" the flavors.

To serve julep, fill each silver julep cup ½ full with shaved ice; insert a mint sprig. Pack in more ice to about 1 inch over top of each cup. Insert straw that has been cut to no more than 1 inch from above top of cup so nose is forced to sniff the "bloom" when sipping julep. When frost forms on cup, pour refrigerated julep mixture over ice and sprinkle powdered sugar on top, if desired. You have made a perfect mint julep the Bill Samuels way.

# RACEHORSE TARTS

### Crust

1½ cups flour

Dash of salt

1 teaspoon sugar

½ cup solid vegetable shortening

⅓ cup ice water

1 egg yolk

### Filling

½ cup flour

1 cup sugar

2 eggs, beaten

¼ pound (1 stick) butter, melted

½ cup pecans

1 cup chocolate chips

1 teaspoon vanilla extract

Bourbon

Preheat oven to 350 degrees.

**To make crust,** mix flour, salt, and sugar. Cut in shortening with pastry cutter until it reaches crumb stage. Beat egg yolk with ice water and add to mixture 1 tablespoon at a time. Press into miniature muffin pans.

**To make filling,** mix flour and sugar and add eggs and melted butter. Add pecans, chocolate chips, and vanilla extract. Pour into shells and bake for 20 minutes. Brush tarts with bourbon while hot.

*Yield:* 3 dozen miniature tarts

# A KENTUCKY WHISKEY CAKE

1 pound maraschino cherries, cut in half

½ pound golden raisins

1 pint Kentucky bourbon whiskey

¾ pound (3 sticks) unsalted butter

2½ cups granulated sugar

2½ cups light brown sugar (packed)

6 eggs, separated

5 cups flour

2 teaspoons ground nutmeg

1 teaspoon baking powder

1 pound pecans

Soak cherries and raisins in bourbon about 8 hours. Cream butter, granulated sugar, and brown sugar until fluffy. Add egg yolks and beat well. Add soaked fruit, remaining bourbon, and flour, reserving small amount of flour for nuts. Add butter mixture. Add nutmeg and baking powder. Beat egg whites until stiff and fold in. Dust pecans with remaining flour and add to mixture.

Bake in large, greased tube pan for 3 to 4 hours at 250 to 275 degrees until a toothpick comes out clean. Do not overbake. When thoroughly cool, loosen sides with knife and turn out. Stuff center hole with cheesecloth soaked in bourbon and store in lightly covered container.

*Yield:* 10 servings

# BISCUIT PUDDING WITH
# JIM BEAM BOURBON SAUCE

*Kurtz Restaurant*

*Kurtz's opened in 1937 and continues to offer fine dining to its many customers. Everything is homemade, down to the great pies.*

### Pudding
1 cup raisins

3 tablespoons Jim Beam bourbon

12 (1½-inch) biscuits

1 quart whole milk

6 eggs

2 cups sugar

2 tablespoons vanilla extract

2 tablespoons butter, melted

### Bourbon Sauce
¼ pound (1 stick) butter

1 cup sugar

¼ cup water

1 egg

⅓ cup Jim Beam bourbon or more, if desired

Soak raisins in bourbon about 8 hours.

Preheat oven to 350 degrees.

Break up biscuits into small pieces and put in large bowl. Add milk and allow to soak for 5 minutes. Beat eggs with sugar and vanilla extract and add to bread mixture. Pour butter and then biscuit mixture into 2-quart baking dish. Bake for 1 hour, until set. Serve warm with bourbon sauce.

**To make bourbon sauce,** melt butter in heavy saucepan. Add sugar and water and cook over medium heat for 5 minutes, stirring occasionally. In separate bowl, beat egg. Remove butter mixture from heat. Gradually add to egg, whisking constantly. Add bourbon and serve.

*Yield:* 10 to 12 servings

# ∞ RIVERBOAT PIE ∞

### Filling
1 cup light brown sugar (packed)

3 eggs, slightly beaten

1 cup light corn syrup

1 teaspoon vanilla extract

2 tablespoons butter, melted

Dash of salt

1½ cups chopped pecans

1 (9-inch) pie shell, unbaked

### Topping
1 cup light whipping cream

1 tablespoon powdered sugar, sifted

1 tablespoon light rum

Preheat oven to 400 degrees.

Blend together brown sugar, eggs, corn syrup, vanilla extract, butter, and salt. Add pecans. Pour into pie shell and bake for 10 minutes. Reduce heat to 325 degrees and bake for 30 to 35 more minutes.

**To make topping,** whip cream with powdered sugar and rum. Serve a dollop on each slice of pie.

*Yield:* 8 servings

# SOUTHERN SWEET POTATO PIE

4 tablespoons (½ stick) butter

½ teaspoon salt

¾ cup sugar

3 egg yolks

Juice of 1 lemon (about 3 tablespoons)

2 teaspoons grated lemon rind

¼ teaspoon ground cinnamon

¼ teaspoon ground nutmeg

¼ teaspoon ground allspice

2 cups mashed sweet potatoes

1 cup whole milk, scalded

3 egg whites, stiffly beaten

1 (9-inch) pie shell, unbaked

Heat oven to 425 degrees.

Blend butter, salt, and sugar. Add egg yolks, lemon juice and rind, cinnamon, nutmeg, allspice, sweet potatoes, and hot milk. Fold in egg whites. Pour into pie shell and bake for 10 minutes. Reduce heat to 350 degrees and continue baking for 30 to 40 minutes, until firm in center. This pie is also excellent topped with a meringue.

*Yield:* 8 servings

# SAWDUST PIE

*Depot Restaurant*

**Pie Shell**

1½ cups flour
1 teaspoon salt
½ cup lard or solid vegetable shortening
½ teaspoon white vinegar
¼ cup water

**Filling**

1½ cups sugar
¾ cup flaked coconut
¾ cup chopped pecans
1½ cups fine graham cracker crumbs
7 egg whites
1 medium banana, sliced
Whipped cream

**To make pie shell,** mix all ingredients until smooth dough forms. Roll out to about ⅛ inch thick on floured surface. Place in pie pan and trim edges.

Preheat oven to 325 degrees.

**To make filling,** mix sugar, coconut, pecans, and cracker crumbs together and add beaten egg whites. Mix well. Pour into unbaked pie shell and bake for 30 to 40 minutes. Top with sliced banana mixed with whipped cream.

*Yield:* 8 servings

# WILD TURKEY RACEHORSE PIE

*Wild Turkey Distillery*

¼ pound (1 stick) margarine, melted

1 cup sugar

½ cup flour

2 eggs, beaten

1 teaspoon Wild Turkey bourbon

¾ cup nuts, soaked in ¼ cup bourbon about 8 hours

¾ cup chocolate chips

1 (9-inch) pie shell, unbaked

Preheat oven to 350 degrees.

Mix ingredients and pour into pie shell. Bake for 30 minutes, or until firm.

*Yield:* 8 servings

*Note:* This pie is excellent served warm. Top with real whipped cream and drizzle with Wild Turkey bourbon.

# Holiday Favorites

# Holiday Favorites

 One day when my daughter, Noélle, was only four, she and I were preparing cookies for our family. As we listened to Christmas carols I sat her up on the island of our large kitchen and let her ice and decorate everything in sight. She was busy putting eyes on a gingerbread person when she pointed the pastry tube at me and asked quite matter-of-factly, "Why did you name me Noélle?"

"It's always been my favorite girl's name," I answered.

She thought for a moment, and, without raising her eyes to look at me, she said with obvious impatience, "You didn't do it because of Christmas, right?"

"No," I said. "It had nothing to do with Christmas."

Finally she raised her head and said with a frown, "Why didn't you just name me Trick or Treat?"

I've lived in many states across the country and have enjoyed the holidays immensely in one or two of them. But nothing compares with

Christmastime in Kentucky. I'm sure most of my fellow Kentuckians would agree. Much of what makes our holidays so special is the food we prepare. Kentucky cooks love to bake or prepare their favorite dishes for a holiday potluck dinner at church or a progressive dinner served in several friends' homes.

For years I marveled at the way my mother-in-law, Flossie Fulkerson Lewis, would prepare divinity on one special day in December. It never failed to turn out perfect, though she was particularly careful not to prepare it on a rainy day, when the humidity would be too high. So much love and tradition went into our annual "divinity days." My kids looked forward to the event even though none of them are particularly fond of divinity. Such happens when Kentucky tradition in the kitchen is present.

I entertain small groups during the holidays and have collected quite an assortment of holiday recipes. Rum Raisin Holiday Spread and my own version of tiramisù are among my favorites, as well as the traditional Christmas Cake. Shaker Village of Pleasant Hill offers us a wonderful Woodford Pudding with a great Vanilla Sauce. In true Shaker style it is a delicious, simple ending to a lavish holiday meal.

Each holiday season, take the opportunity to appreciate the bounty of the bluegrass, your own culinary talents, and the traditions and aromas of the season found only in Kentucky.

# BANANA PUNCH

6 to 8 medium bananas
1 (6-ounce) can frozen lemonade, thawed
1 (12-ounce) can frozen orange juice, thawed
3 cups warm water
2 cups sugar
1 (46-ounce) can pineapple juice
3 (2-liter) bottles lemon lime soda

Blend bananas, lemonade, and orange juice. Divide the blended juice into 2 parts and add 1½ cups water and 1 cup sugar to each. Put in containers with lids and freeze. Remove from freezer 1 hour before serving. Place all the frozen blended juice in a large punch bowl and add pineapple juice and soda.

*Yield:* 16 to 20 servings
*Note:* Float banana slices on top for a nice touch.

# CHAMPAGNE HOLIDAY PUNCH

4 cups cranberry juice cocktail
1 cup water
½ of a 6-ounce can orange juice concentrate
6 inches of stick cinnamon
1 (750-milliliter) bottle champagne, chilled

Combine cranberry juice cocktail, water, orange juice concentrate, and cinnamon sticks in large saucepan. Bring to a boil and boil uncovered for 5 minutes. Strain, cover, and chill. Just before serving, pour cranberry mixture into punch bowl. Gradually pour chilled champagne down side of bowl, stirring gently.

*Yield:* 18 half-cup servings

# ∽ EGGNOG ∽

*Maker's Mark Distillery, from* That Special Touch *by Sandra Davis*

24 eggs

1½ cups sugar

1 liter Maker's Mark bourbon

1 quart heavy whipping cream

1 quart milk

Freshly grated nutmeg for garnish

Separate eggs and beat yolks until creamy. Whip sugar into yolks. Beat egg whites until they stand in peaks, adding ½ cup additional sugar, if needed. Beat yolks and bourbon together and fold in whites. Beat cream and add with milk. Serve in eggnog cups. Add nutmeg for garnish.

*Yield:* 1 punch bowl-full

# ∽ BUTTERMILK PRALINES ∽

1 cup buttermilk

2 cups sugar

Pinch of salt

1 teaspoon baking soda

⅓ stick unsalted butter

2 teaspoons vanilla extract

2½ cups pecans, chopped

Mix buttermilk, sugar, salt, and baking soda. Stir and cook in saucepan to 235 degrees on candy thermometer (soft ball stage). Add butter and vanilla extract. Beat with electric mixer for 1 minute, until mixture begins to thicken. Add pecans and mix. Drop onto buttered waxed paper and cool.

*Yield:* 2 dozen

# CHOCOLATE-COVERED CHERRIES

1 pound quality dark chocolate

2 to 3 tablespoons melted paraffin

3½ cups powdered sugar

2 tablespoons evaporated milk

1 teaspoon vanilla extract

1 large jar maraschino cherries with stems,
drained and dried with paper towel

In top of double boiler, melt chocolate over medium heat. Blend in paraffin. In bowl, mix together powdered sugar, evaporated milk, and vanilla extract. Wrap a spoonful of sugar mixture around each cherry, leaving stem uncovered. Dip into chocolate mixture to coat. Cool on waxed paper-lined cookie sheet. Place cooled candy in petit four cups.

*Yield:* about 2 dozen

# BAKED FUDGE PUDDING

2 eggs

1 cup sugar

2 tablespoons flour

2 tablespoons cocoa

¼ pound (1 stick) butter, melted

½ cup chopped pecans

1 teaspoon vanilla extract

Dash of salt

Whipped cream

Preheat oven to 300 degrees.

In large bowl beat eggs with sugar, flour, and cocoa. Mix well. Add butter, pecans, vanilla extract, and salt. Pour into 6 ramekins (individual baking dishes) and bake in pan of hot water for 50 minutes. Refrigerate for several hours and serve with whipped cream.

*Yield:* 6 servings

# HOLIDAY PUDDING

6 egg yolks

1 cup sugar

1 cup burgundy or port wine

1 envelope (1 tablespoon) unflavored gelatin,
softened in ½ cup cold water

1 cup fine vanilla wafer crumbs

1 cup chopped pecans

6 egg whites, stiffly beaten

In saucepan, mix together egg yolks and sugar, stirring until well blended. Whisk in wine slowly to avoid cooking egg yolks. Cook over low heat, stirring constantly, until thickened. Cool slightly and stir in softened gelatin until well blended. Add vanilla wafer crumbs and pecans. Fold in egg whites.

Mixture may be divided into individual serving dishes at this point or turned into pretty crystal bowl. Refrigerate at least several hours before serving. May be made several days ahead. When ready to serve, top with sweetened whipped cream.

*Yield:* 8 servings

## ∞ PUDDING NOÉLLE ∞

*I named this holiday pudding for my daughter. It's always a hit, truly Kentucky, and very festive, just like my Noélle.*

1 envelope (1 tablespoon) unflavored gelatin
2 tablespoons cold water
¼ cup milk
2 eggs, separated
½ cup sugar
¼ cup good Kentucky bourbon
2 cups heavy whipping cream, whipped
12 ladyfingers, split
Finely chopped pecans

Soak gelatin in the cold water. Bring milk to a boil and pour over gelatin. Beat egg whites until very stiff. Beat yolks, adding sugar and bourbon. Add softened gelatin and beaten egg whites. Fold in half of whipped cream. Pour pudding into bowl lined with 12 of the ladyfinger halves. Top with remaining ladyfinger halves. Chill for several hours, or until set. Turn out onto serving plate. Spread remaining whipped cream on top and sprinkle with chopped pecans.

*Yield:* 8 servings

# WOODFORD PUDDING
## WITH VANILLA SAUCE

*Shaker Village of Pleasant Hill*
*From* We Make You Kindly Welcome *by Elizabeth C. Kremer*

**Pudding**
¼ pound (1 stick) butter
1 cup flour
1 teaspoon baking soda
1 full teaspoon cinnamon
1 cup sugar
1 cup blackberry jam
½ cup sour milk
3 eggs

**Vanilla Sauce**
½ cup sugar
1 tablespoon cornstarch
1 cup boiling water
1 teaspoon vanilla extract
2 tablespoons butter
Few grains nutmeg
Few grains salt

Mix all pudding ingredients together well. Bake in pudding dish at 375 degrees for 40 minutes, or until lightly firm.

**To make sauce,** mix sugar and cornstarch. Gradually add the boiling water. Boil 5 minutes. Remove from heat and add other ingredients. Serve hot.

*Yield:* 6 servings

# ❧ JAM CAKE ❧

*Cissy Gregg, from* The Courier-Journal Cookbook

*This is a 1984 version of Cissy Gregg's recipe for a Kentucky favorite. It doesn't read like Cissy, so obviously it's been boiled down and polished up over the years.*

6 eggs, beaten

½ pound (2 sticks) butter, melted

4 tablespoons buttermilk

2 cups brown sugar

1 cup blackberry jam

3 cups flour

1 teaspoon baking soda

2 teaspoons ground cinnamon

2 teaspoons ground allspice

2 teaspoons ground nutmeg

1 cup English walnuts or pecans, chopped

1 cup raisins

Bourbon

Preheat oven to 325 degrees.

Mix eggs with melted butter, buttermilk, brown sugar, and blackberry jam. Sift flour with baking soda, cinnamon, allspice and nutmeg. Add to egg mixture and mix well. Fold in nuts and raisins. Pour into greased and floured 9-inch tube pan. Bake for 1½ to 2 hours. Let cool slightly, about 5 minutes, and turn out on cake rack. While still warm, drizzle bourbon on bottom and lightly pierce with fork so bourbon will seep down into middle of cake.

*Yield:* 12 servings

# ❦ CHRISTMAS CAKE ❦ WITH BROWN SUGAR ICING

*There are many lovely alternatives to the traditional fruitcake. This is indeed one of them.*

### Cake
½ pound (2 sticks) butter

2 cups sugar

1 teaspoon vanilla extract

3 eggs

1 teaspoon baking soda

1 cup buttermilk

3 cups flour

Dash of salt

1 teaspoon baking powder

1 teaspoon ground cinnamon

½ teaspoon ground cloves

¼ teaspoon ground allspice

1 cup stewed apples, sweetened, or mashed apple pie filling

1 (4- to 6-ounce) bottle maraschino cherries, drained and chopped

1 cup nuts, chopped (I use pecans)

### Brown Sugar Icing
3 cups light brown sugar

1 cup granulated sugar

1½ cups milk

6 tablespoons butter

2 teaspoons vanilla extract

Preheat oven to 350 degrees.

In mixing bowl, cream butter and sugar. Add vanilla extract. Add eggs one at a time, beating well after each. Add baking soda to buttermilk. Sift flour, salt, baking powder, cinnamon, cloves, and allspice. Add to butter mixture, alternating with buttermilk. Mix until well blended. Fold in apples, cherries, and nuts. Pour batter into 3 greased and floured 8-inch cake pans. Bake for 20 to 25 minutes, until toothpick inserted comes out clean.

**To make icing**, combine sugars, milk, and butter. Cook over medium heat, stirring constantly, to 242 degrees. Remove from heat and add vanilla extract. Beat until mixture is of spreading consistency and frost cake immediately. Icing will harden on cake; add more milk if it hardens too fast.

*Yield:* 12 servings

# WHISKEY CAKE

*My Old Kentucky Home State Park*

*My Old Kentucky Home State Park in Bardstown, Kentucky, is
known throughout the world because of the beautiful song written
by Stephen Foster. The song "My Old Kentucky Home" was inspired
by Foster's cousins' plantation, Federal Hill,
which is the focal point of the park.
This cake is served during tours of My Old Kentucky Home State
Park, where costumed guides tell the story of the prominent Rowan
family as they take you through the home, the gardens, the carriage
house, and the smokehouse. The Christmas tour is another of several
spectacular events here each year during the holidays.*

## Cake
1 (2-ounce) package vanilla pudding mix

1 package yellow cake mix

4 eggs

½ cup oil

½ cup water

1 cup nuts

## Topping
¼ cup water

½ cup whiskey

¼ pound (1 stick) butter

1 cup sugar

Preheat oven to 350 degrees.

Combine pudding mix, cake mix, eggs, oil, and water and mix until smooth. Add nuts. Pour into 13 x 9 x 2-inch pan. Bake for 40 to 45 minutes.

**To make topping,** mix all ingredients and bring to hard boil; boil for 3 or 4 minutes. Pour over hot cake while still in pan. Cool before removing from pan.

*Yield:* 12 servings

## ∞ PUMPKIN CRUNCH ∞

*White Pillars Bed and Breakfast*

*White Pillars Bed and Breakfast in Russell Springs, Kentucky, is located in a traditional southern home built in 1876. Its recipe for Pumpkin Crunch is a favorite of many.*

2 cups cooked and mashed pumpkin

12 ounces evaporated milk

3 eggs, lightly beaten

1 cup sugar

4 teaspoons pumpkin pie spice

½ teaspoon salt

1 yellow butter cake mix

1 cup quick-cook oats or 1 cup chopped nuts

½ pound (2 sticks) butter, melted

Preheat oven to 350 degrees.

Mix pumpkin, evaporated milk, eggs, sugar, pumpkin pie spice, and salt together. Pour into buttered 13 x 9 x 2-inch cake pan. Sprinkle dry cake mix and oats or nuts over top. Pour melted butter over top of mixture. Bake for 50 to 60 minutes. Serve warm, with whipped topping if desired.

*Yield:* 12 servings

# FRUITCAKE COOKIES

½ pound (1 carton) candied cherries

3 (8-ounce) boxes dates

½ pound (1 carton) candied pineapple

4 cups chopped pecans

2½ cups flour

1 teaspoon salt

1 teaspoon baking soda

1 teaspoon ground cinnamon

½ pound (2 sticks) margarine

1½ cups sugar

2 eggs, well beaten

Preheat oven to 350 degrees.

Chop cherries, dates, pineapple, and pecans. Sift together flour, salt, baking soda, and cinnamon. Cream margarine until fluffy and add sugar and eggs. Combine all ingredients and mix well. Drop by teaspoonfuls onto ungreased cookie sheet and bake for about 8 minutes until light brown for chewy cookies or 10 minutes for darker, crisp cookies.

*Yield:* 4-5 dozen cookies

# SPRITZ COOKIES

1 cup sugar

½ pound (2 sticks) butter

1 egg, beaten

2 cups flour, sifted

1 teaspoon almond extract

Preheat oven to 400 degrees.

Cream sugar and butter together until light and fluffy. Blend in egg. Add flour and almond flavoring and mix well. Using cookie press, place cookies 1½ inches apart. Bake for 10 to 14 minutes, until light brown around edges.

*Yield:* 6 dozen cookies

## ⧉ SPUMONI MERINGUES ⧉

*I must admit that I go to great lengths to create spectacular dishes during the holidays to serve to my family and closest friends. This is so simple, yet so elegant. If you love spumoni ice cream as much as I do, you'll love this holiday dessert. Kids certainly do!*

**Meringue shells**

3 egg whites

1 teaspoon vanilla extract

¼ teaspoon cream of tartar

Dash of salt

1 cup sugar

1 pint spumoni ice cream

Fine graham cracker crumbs

Have egg whites at room temperature. Add vanilla extract, cream of tartar, and salt. Beat until frothy. Gradually add sugar, a little at a time, beating until very stiff peaks form and sugar is dissolved. Cover cookie sheet with waxed paper. Using large pastry bag with tube, form 5 meringues by filling in a circle and building up sides to make a "cup" to hold ice cream. Use ½ cup mixture for each meringue. Heat oven to 275 degrees and bake for 1 hour. Let dry in oven for 1 additional hour. Fill cooled meringues with ice cream and sprinkle with graham cracker crumbs.

# TIRAMISÙ

*Tiramisù is an incredible Italian dessert made with rich mascarpone cheese, espresso, and Grand Marnier. There are many wonderful versions, but this is my favorite.*

4 egg yolks

½ cup sugar

1 pound mascarpone cheese, softened

34 ladyfingers

¼ cup Grand Marnier liqueur

1¼ cups cold espresso

Cocoa powder

Beat egg yolks until light and fluffy. Add sugar slowly and continue beating until sugar is dissolved and mixture is very pale in color. Add cheese gradually and continue beating until mixture is creamy and completely smooth. Arrange half of ladyfingers in square pan side by side, completely covering dish bottom. Mix Grand Marnier with espresso. Spoon half of cold Grand Marnier mixture evenly over ladyfingers.

Spread half of cheese mixture over ladyfingers, covering completely. Repeat layering process with ladyfingers, Grand Marnier mix, and cheese mixture. After second layer is complete sprinkle with cocoa powder and chill thoroughly. Cut into 8 pieces with spatula and serve.

*Yield:* 8 servings

# WARM CIDER SAUCE

1 cup apple cider

¾ cup light corn syrup

¼ cup sugar

4 tablespoons (½ stick) butter

Juice (about 3 tablespoons) and grated rind of 1 lemon

½ teaspoon ground nutmeg

Pinch of ground ginger

Combine all ingredients in saucepan and heat until sugar dissolves. Serve warm.

*Yield:* About 2 cups

*Note:* This is great on pumpkin, mince, or apple pie, ice cream, or apple dumplings. It refrigerates well and may be reheated in microwave.

## ∞ PRETZEL SALAD ∞

2 cups crushed pretzels

1¼ cups sugar

1¼ sticks margarine

8 ounces whipped cream cheese

1 cup whipped topping

2 cups pineapple juice

2 (3-ounce) packages strawberry gelatin

2 (10-ounce) packages frozen strawberries

Preheat oven to 350 degrees.

Mix pretzels, ¼ cup of the sugar, and margarine. Spray 13 x 9 x 2-inch pan with cooking spray and spread pretzel mixture in it. Bake for 10 minutes. Allow to cool completely. Mix cream cheese, the remaining 1 cup sugar, and whipped topping and spread over baked pretzel mixture. Heat pineapple juice and dissolve gelatin in it. Add frozen strawberries and cool until gelatin just begins to set. Spread over cream cheese layer and refrigerate until solid. Cut into squares and serve on bed of lettuce.

*Yield:* 8 servings

# CHERRY CHIP NUT BREAD WITH CHERRY SPREAD

**Bread**

2½ cups flour

1 cup buttermilk

1 cup chopped pecans

½ cup granulated sugar

½ cup light brown sugar (firmly packed)

2 eggs, beaten

4 tablespoons (½ stick) butter, softened

¼ cup maraschino cherry juice

1 tablespoon baking powder

½ teaspoon salt

½ teaspoon baking soda

½ cup chopped, drained maraschino cherries

**Cherry Spread**

4 ounces cream cheese, softened

4 tablespoons (½ stick) butter or margarine, softened

½ cup cherry preserves

1 tablespoon kirsch or other cherry-flavored liqueur (optional)

Preheat oven to 350 degrees.

Combine all bread ingredients except cherries in mixing bowl. Blend on low speed of electric mixer for 15 seconds; increase to medium speed and continue blending for 30 more seconds. Fold in cherries.

Pour batter into greased and floured 9 x 5 x 3-inch loaf pan. Bake for 1 hour and 10 to 15 minutes, or until toothpick inserted in center comes out clean. Cool for 10 minutes in pan and remove to wire rack to cool completely. Serve with Cherry Spread.

**To make spread,** beat cream cheese and butter at medium speed until smooth. Add preserves and liqueur, if using. Cover and refrigerate.

*Yield:* 1 loaf


## ∞ RUM RAISIN ∞ HOLIDAY SPREAD

1½ cups raisins

5 tablespoons dark rum

½ pound sharp cheddar cheese, finely grated (2 cups)

6 ounces cream cheese

Soak raisins in rum until plump.

In food processor, process cheeses until smooth and spreadable. Add raisins and rum and blend well.

*Yield:* 2 cups

*Note:* Serve with sweet quick breads and fruit.

# ZUCCHINI BREAD

3 eggs

1 cup vegetable oil

2 cups sugar

2 cups grated zucchini

3 cups flour

¼ teaspoon baking powder

1 tablespoon baking soda

1 teaspoon salt

Dash of ground nutmeg

1 teaspoon ground cinnamon

½ cup chopped nuts

Preheat oven to 350 degrees. Beat eggs in large bowl. Add oil, sugar, and zucchini. Sift together flour, baking powder, baking soda, salt, nutmeg, and cinnamon and add to zucchini mixture. Stir in nuts. Pour into greased loaf pan. Bake for 1 hour, or until toothpick inserted in center comes out clean.

*Yield:* 1 loaf

# CRABMEAT AND ZUCCHINI BREAD SANDWICHES

6 ounces fresh or frozen fully cooked crabmeat

2 ounces crème fraîche (recipe follows)

½ bunch snipped fresh chives

4 slices fresh zucchini bread

Watercress for garnish

Toss crabmeat with crème fraîche and chives. Thinly slice zucchini bread and remove crusts. Layer 2 slices of bread with crabmeat mixture. Top with remaining slices. Cut in half diagonally and garnish with fresh watercress.

*Yield:* 4 sandwiches

# CRÈME FRAÎCHE

1 cup heavy cream

2 tablespoons sour cream

Mix and let thicken 8 hours at room temperature. Store in refrigerator. Will keep 2 weeks.

*Note:* Can also be used on fruits and desserts.

# CHEESE WAFERS

*Shaker Village of Pleasant Hill*
*From* We Make You Kindly Welcome *by Elizabeth C. Kremer*

*Shaker Village of Pleasant Hill is a living legacy of good food,*
*gracious hospitality, and the peaceful way of life enjoyed*
*by a Shaker colony who settled here in 1805.*
*Their lasting influence is evident to all who visit Pleasant Hill.*

½ pound (2 sticks) butter, softened

2 cups flour

½ pound sharp cheddar cheese, grated (2 cups)

1 egg, beaten

Whole pecans

Mix butter, flour, and cheese all together with your hands; then roll out on floured board and cut with a very small biscuit cutter. Place on cookie sheet and brush tops with beaten egg. Put pecan on top of each and bake at 350 degrees for 10 minutes. As soon as you take them out of the oven, sprinkle them with salt and remove them from the cookie sheet.

*Yield:* About 75 wafers

# ❦ MY FAVORITE ❦ WHITE BREAD DRESSING

*I believe the reason my dressing is so rich and good is that I primarily use only the cooked broth from the turkey, adding canned chicken broth only when there isn't enough turkey broth. There are holidays when I add fresh oysters with their liquid or chopped apples (one or two) with a pound of cooked, crumbled pork sausage, but this is my basic recipe and the one I serve most of the time. The only drawback was that my kids, when they were younger, always wanted to eat spoonfuls of it before it was baked. I wonder if they realized it had raw eggs in it. Somehow I don't think that would have stopped them. But that was way back before we knew about salmonella.*

1½ loaves toasted white bread, torn into chunks

1 cup chopped onions

1 cup chopped celery

1½ sticks unsalted butter

1 teaspoon sage

2 eggs, lightly beaten

1 teaspoon salt

½ teaspoon pepper

Broth from cooked turkey

Put bread in large baking dish. Sauté onions and celery in butter until translucent. Add sage and pour over bread. Combine eggs, salt, and pepper and mix with bread mixture. When turkey is almost done, pour off broth and add enough so that dressing will be quite moist but not soupy. Cover dressing and bake for 40 minutes in 350-degree oven. Remove cover and bake an additional 5 minutes.

*Yield:* 16 servings

# MY HOLIDAY ASPARAGUS CASSEROLE

*My traditional Thanksgiving dinner would not be complete without this wonderful casserole. Even those who don't like asparagus love this.*

2 tablespoons unsalted butter

3 tablespoons flour

1 teaspoon salt

¼ teaspoon pepper

1½ cups 2 percent milk

1 egg, divided

3 ounces cheddar cheese, grated (¾ cup)

1 pound frozen or canned asparagus, drained and cut into 1-inch pieces

½ cup crumbs of buttery round crackers

Preheat oven to 350 degrees.

Make cream sauce using butter, flour, salt, pepper, milk, and egg yolk. Cook over medium heat, stirring constantly. After mixture begins to thicken, add half of cheese. Pour mixture into buttered 1½-quart casserole and add asparagus pieces. Stir gently. Beat egg white until stiff and gently fold into casserole. Sprinkle with cracker crumbs and bake for 20 to 25 minutes, until lightly browned.

*Yield:* 8 servings

# CRANBERRY RELISH

*Ditto House*

2 cups cranberries
1 orange, peeled and seeded
Rind from ½ orange
1 cup apples, peeled and cored
¼ cup nuts
¾ cup sugar

Grind cranberries, orange, orange rind, apples, and nuts. Add sugar and stir well. Chill.

*Yield:* 8 servings
*Note:* This relish freezes well.

# FRIED CORNMEAL MUSH

*When I was a child, the sight of white cornmeal mush "setting" in the refrigerator brought promise of a wonderful breakfast the next morning. Fried cornmeal mush was an occasional dish, but one we all looked forward to.*

1 teaspoon salt
3 cups water
⅔ cup white cornmeal
Flour for dredging
Vegetable oil for frying

Add salt to 3 cups water and bring to a boil in heavy saucepan over medium heat. Sprinkle cornmeal into water, stirring constantly. After mixture becomes thick, reduce heat and cook 45 minutes longer, stirring occasionally. Remove from heat and pour into greased loaf pan. Smooth surface with spatula. Chill for several hours, until very firm. Slice ¾ inch thick and dredge slices in flour. Brown in skillet in hot oil and serve with melted butter and maple syrup.

*Yield:* 8 servings

# Bluegrass Bounty

# Bluegrass Bounty

 My friend Linda recalls visiting her grandma Josie in Rhodelia, Kentucky, some forty years ago. Linda would "help" her grandmother can and preserve the produce from the family garden. One summer day, Linda was helping by collecting jars from the storage shed. As she passed the old tree in the yard, the five-year-old noticed "pickles" on the ground. She collected them and canned them, placing them in the attic of the old house, next to the window so the jars would sparkle in the sun the way her grandmother's did. Several months later, her grandfather found the jars of her "pickles," which were actually pods from the tree that had rotted and smelled awful.

We are blessed to live in a state where fruits and vegetables abound during warm months. I prefer Kentucky tomatoes over any other, and I make full use of a garden whenever I can. I have canned for years, but still get excited over new jam recipes or how beautiful green beans look when I put the jars on the shelves. When Christian and Andrea (my son and beautiful daughter-in-law) visit from Cincinnati we love to enjoy a jar of homemade strawberry or blackberry preserves with breakfast.

I will never forget how amazed I was the first time I made bread and butter pickles. I couldn't believe they could taste so much better than any variety I had tried from the supermarket. Watermelons could become pickles and green tomatoes made wonderful relish. Chutney could be eaten any time during the year, and I had found a new love for cooking. It certainly is time consuming, but so much worth the effort to preserve for cold winter days the bounty of our gardens or bushels purchased at local farmers' markets. When time allows, try some of these exciting recipes.

*Note:* When canning, unless directions specify otherwise, pack prepared fruits or vegetables in clean, hot jars and fill with liquid to ½ inch from top of jar. Place lids on jars and tighten. Process jars in boiling water bath for time specified in recipe and remove jars. When jars have cooled to lukewarm (to the touch), give lids one last twist to tighten and watch (and listen for pop) for lids to seal. Store in cool, dry place.

# APPLE BUTTER

*Apple Butter is a favorite at my house on cold mornings.*
*It's delicious with hot biscuits.*

½ bushel apples

4 pounds sugar

2 tablespoons ground cinnamon

¼ teaspoon ground allspice

½ teaspoon salt

¼ cup red hots

Peel, core, and quarter apples. Cook in Dutch oven over low heat until tender. Juice will form.

Preheat oven to 325 degrees.

Transfer applesauce to large roaster and add remaining ingredients. Blend well. Bake uncovered, stirring occasionally, until thick. Pack in jars and process 5 minutes in boiling water bath to seal.

*Yield:* about 10 pints
*Note:* The red hots add flavor and color to the butter.


# APRICOT-PINEAPPLE JAM

2 (15-ounce) cans apricots, drained and diced

4 cups sugar

1 (16-ounce) can crushed pineapple, drained

Combine apricots and sugar. Stir over low heat until sugar is dissolved. Boil for 20 minutes. Add drained pineapple and return to a boil. Pour into hot, sterilized jars and seal.

*Yield:* 3 pints

# BANANA PEPPERS

2 gallons water

3 cups salt

Banana peppers

1 cup cider vinegar

1 teaspoon alum per jar

Put 1 gallon water, 2 cups of the salt, and banana peppers in large crock. Use as many peppers as the water will cover. Place weight on top and let sit for 24 hours.

Drain and pack peppers in jars. Bring to a boil 1 gallon water, vinegar, and the remaining 1 cup salt. Fill packed jars with vinegar mixture. Add 1 teaspoon alum to each jar. Process in water bath for 5 minutes. Seal.

*Yield:* about 8 to 10 quarts

# CAULIFLOWER PICKLES

1 tablespoon salt.

3 large heads cauliflower, florets only

3 pints white vinegar

3½ cups sugar

¼ cup pickling spices, tied in cheesecloth

4 hot red peppers

Sprinkle salt over cauliflower and let stand for 12 hours. Rinse thoroughly in colander. Bring vinegar, sugar, and spice bag to a boil and continue boiling for 5 minutes. Add cauliflower and boil 2 minutes longer. Remove spice bag and pack pickles in sterile jars, reserving liquid. Add liquid to within ½ inch of top of jars. Put 1 hot red pepper in each jar and seal.

*Yield:* 8 quarts

# DILLED GREEN BEANS

4 pounds whole tender green beans (4 quarts)

¼ teaspoon crushed red pepper per pint jar

½ teaspoon whole mustard seed per pint jar

½ teaspoon dill seed per pint jar

1 clove garlic per pint jar

5 cups white vinegar

5 cups water

½ cup salt

Wash beans thoroughly. Cut into lengths to fit pint jars. Pack beans into clean, hot jars and add crushed red pepper, mustard seed, dill seed, and garlic. Combine vinegar, water, and salt. Heat to boiling. Pour boiling liquid over beans, filling to within ½ inch of top of jars. Place lids on jars and tighten. Process in boiling water for 5 minutes. Seal.

*Yield:* 7 pints


# PEACH BUTTER

5 pounds fresh peaches

5 cups sugar

Juice and grated rind of 1 small orange

2 teaspoons ground cinnamon

1 teaspoon ground cloves

¾ teaspoon ground allspice

Wash, peel, and remove pits from peaches. Cut into small pieces. Add sugar, orange juice, and rind. Stir until sugar is dissolved and add cinnamon, cloves, and allspice. Simmer over low heat, stirring often, until mixture thickens to spreadable consistency. Pour into hot, sterilized jars and seal.

*Yield:* 6 pints

# PEACH-ORANGE MARMALADE

About 4 pounds peaches (5 cups finely chopped or ground)

About 2 medium-size oranges (1 cup finely chopped or ground)

Peel of 1 orange, finely grated

2 tablespoons lemon juice

6 cups sugar

Wash, peel, and remove pits from peaches. Finely chop or grind peaches. Remove peel, white portion, and seeds from oranges. Finely chop or grind pulp. Measure prepared fruit into large pot. Add remaining ingredients, stir well, and bring to a boil. Boil rapidly, stirring constantly, until mixture thickens. Remove from heat and skim surface. Fill and seal jars. Process for 5 minutes in boiling water bath.

*Yield:* 7 half-pint jars

# PEAR HONEY

7 pounds fresh pears

7 cups sugar

1 (16-ounce) can crushed pineapple, drained

1 cup flaked coconut

Wash, core, and peel pears. Grind coarsely. Mix pears and sugar and cook in large heavy pot until thick. Add pineapple and again cook until thick. Add coconut and mix well. Put in jars and seal.

*Yield:* 10 pints

## PRUNE MARMALADE

2 cups water
1 pound dried prunes
1½ cups sugar
⅔ cup juice and grated rind of 2 small oranges

Pour 2 cups water over prunes and let stand about 8 hours. Drain thoroughly, reserving liquid. Remove pits from prunes and chop prunes. Combine prunes, reserved liquid, sugar, orange rind, and juice. In saucepan, bring to a boil; reduce heat and simmer until thick, about 30 minutes. Stir often to prevent scorching. Pack in hot sterilized jars and adjust lids. Process in boiling water bath 5 minutes and seal.

*Yield:* 4 pints

## TOMATO APPLE CHUTNEY

6 pounds tomatoes, peeled and chopped
5 pounds apples, peeled and chopped
2 cups seedless white raisins
2 cups chopped onions (4 medium)
1 cup chopped green peppers (2 medium)
5 cups light brown sugar (packed)
2 teaspoons salt
1 teaspoon ground ginger
¼ cup mixed whole pickling spice

Combine all ingredients except the whole spices. Place the whole spices in a cheesecloth bag, tie with string, and add to tomato-apple mixture. Bring to a boil. Reduce heat and cook slowly, stirring frequently until mixture is thickened, about 1 hour. Remove spice bag. Pack the boiling hot chutney into clean, hot jars to ½ inch of tops. Adjust and tighten lids. Process in water bath for 5 minutes and seal.

*Yield:* 7 pints

# TOMATO GINGER PRESERVES

3 cups cooked and peeled fresh, ripe tomatoes, about 4 medium
1 tablespoon chopped candied ginger
¼ cup lemon juice
1 (1.75-ounce) box Sure Jell
4½ cups sugar

Put tomatoes, ginger, lemon juice, and Sure Jell into 8-quart kettle. Bring to a full boil over high heat, stirring constantly. Continue cooking until mixture reaches a rolling boil that cannot be stirred down. Add sugar and once again bring mixture to a rolling boil that cannot be stirred down. Boil 1 minute more, stirring constantly. Remove from heat and remove foam. Pour into hot sterilized jars and adjust and tighten lids. Process in boiling water bath 5 minutes and seal.

Yield: 4 pints

# TOMATO MARMALADE

3 oranges
2 lemons
4 sticks cinnamon
1 tablespoon whole cloves
3 quarts ripe tomatoes, peeled, chopped, and drained, 10 to 12 medium
6 cups sugar
1 teaspoon salt

Slice oranges and lemons very thin. Quarter the slices. Tie cinnamon and cloves in a cheesecloth bag. Put tomatoes in large kettle. Add sugar and salt and stir until dissolved. Add oranges, lemons, and spice bag. Boil rapidly, stirring constantly, until thick and clear (about 50 minutes). Remove from heat and skim surface. Fill hot sterilized half-pint jars and adjust lids. Process in boiling water bath 5 minutes and seal.

Yield: 9 half-pint jars

# WATERMELON PICKLES

3 quarts (6 pounds) watermelon rind, unpeeled,
or rind from ½ large melon

¾ cup salt

3 quarts cold water

2 quarts (2 trays) ice cubes

1 tablespoon whole cloves

6 (1-inch) pieces stick cinnamon

9 cups sugar

3 cups distilled white vinegar

3 cups water

1 lemon, seeded and thinly sliced

Pare rind and all pink edges from watermelon. Cut rind into 1-inch squares or shapes of your choice. Cover with brine made by mixing salt with 3 quarts cold water in nonmetal container. Add ice cubes. Let stand 5 or 6 hours. Drain and rinse in cold water. Cover with cold water and cook until tender to the fork, about 10 minutes (do not overcook). Drain.

Tie cloves and cinnamon in a cheesecloth bag. Combine sugar, vinegar, water, and spices in saucepan. Boil 5 minutes and then pour over watermelon. Add lemon slices and let stand about 8 hours.

Heat watermelon in its syrup to boiling and cook until watermelon is translucent (about 10 minutes). Pack hot pickles loosely in clean, hot, pint jars. To each jar, add 1 piece of stick cinnamon from spice bag. Cover with the boiling syrup to ½ inch of top of jar. Adjust lids. Process in boiling water bath 5 minutes and seal.

*Yield:* 4 to 5 pints
*Note:* Add green or red food coloring to the syrup, if desired.
Rinds may be stored in plastic bags in the refrigerator
until enough accumulate for 1 batch.

# ❦ ZUCCHINI JAM ❦

3 cups cooked, mashed zucchini, about 3 medium

½ cup water

1 large (6-serving size) box flavored gelatin (any flavor)

¼ cup lemon juice

3 cups sugar

1 (1.75 ounce) box Sure Jell

Peel and chop zucchini. Put in large saucepan and add ½ cup water. Cook over medium heat until tender and mash or stir until texture of crushed pineapple. Measure 3 cups and put in 2½-quart pot. Add gelatin and lemon juice. Boil over medium heat 2 minutes. Pour into hot sterilized jelly jars and adjust lids. Process in boiling water bath 5 minutes and seal.

*Note:* Leftover mashed zuchini may be frozen in freezer bags and used later in quick bread.

# Index